WOMEN AS TEACHERS AND DISCIPLES IN TRADITIONAL AND NEW RELIGIONS

WOMEN AS TEACHERS AND DISCIPLES IN TRADITIONAL AND NEW RELIGIONS

Edited by

Elizabeth Puttick

and

Peter B. Clarke

Studies in Women and Religion
Volume 32

The Edwin Mellen Press
Lewiston/Queenston/Lampeter

Library of Congress Cataloging-in-Publication Data

Women as teachers and disciples in traditional and new religions /
edited by Elizabeth Puttick and Peter B. Clarke.
     p.   cm. -- (Studies in women and religion ; v. 32)
    Includes bibliographical references (p. xxx-xxx) and index.
    ISBN 0-7734-9346-8
    1. Women and religion--Congresses. I. Puttick, Elizabeth, 1952-
. II. Clarke, Peter B. (Peter Bernard) III. Series.
BL458.W5763   1993
291.6'1'082--dc20
                         93-30865
                           CIP

This is volume 32 in the continuing series
Studies in Women and Religion
Volume 32 ISBN 0-7734-9346-8
SWR Series ISBN 0-88946-549-5

A CIP catalog record for this book
is available from the British Library.

Copyright © 1993 The Edwin Mellen Press

The Edwin Mellen Press
Box 450
Lewiston, New York
USA 14092

The Edwin Mellen Press
Box 67
Queenston, Ontario
CANADA L0S 1L0

Edwin Mellen Press, Ltd.
Lampeter, Dyfed, Wales
UNITED KINGDOM SA48 7DY

Printed in the United States of America

Contents

Foreword

The popular image of women is all too often influenced by the artificially created covers of glossy magazines picturing youthful, glamorous women as fashion models and pop stars, an image also widely prevalent in film and television. But real women are hardly ever like that, although some might succumb to the lure of glamour when they slavishly follow the latest fashion and thereby become dependent on an inappropriate and unappropriated lifestyle hardly their own. This kind of following, of 'discipleship' to external cultural fashions, is discipleship in name only. It points to the utter immaturity, lack of independence and vulnerability of women following idols outside themselves. But true discipleship is of quite a different nature. More than external following and imitative dependence it poses deep, challenging questions and leads to autonomy and strong, self-centred but not egocentric, affirmation and relationships.

This is true of all discipleship, but one can ask quite separately, as this book does, how spiritual discipleship affects women in particular. How do they practise it? What attracts them to it? What do they gain through it? If women have been stereotypically identified with the superficial expressions of external physical beauty and artificially produced glamour, men, (though not all men), are traditionally seen as the purveyors of power – social, intellectual, institutional and political – summed up in the domination and abuse of patriarchy in all its forms. Women have been excluded and separated from this form of power. Yet nonetheless theirs has been a power grounded in subtler, more invisible forms, fed by the heart, mind and emotions and, deepest of all, by the wells of the Spirit.

It is impossible to define such spiritual power in its ever-renewing freshness, creativity, inventiveness, abundance, surprise and joy. As the Greek form of the word power – *dunamis* – expresses, such power is dynamic and alive. It is energy in all its forms which gives, nourishes, sustains and transforms life, and heals all its wounds. When we mention the word 'dynamic' we associate it with other descriptions such as energetic, vigorous, active, efficient and efficacious – all words which indicate how much the power of the Spirit is the very opposite of something predictable, unchanging and stagnant. For those whose worldview includes a deep faith in the presence and power of the Spirit, spiritual power is at the very centre of their lives, an ever-renewing source of strength and empowerment. Through the ages countless men and women have followed the call of the Spirit and become disciples seeking the path of salvation, wisdom and enlightenment by following a prophet, teacher or guru with a message speaking to their heart.

All religious traditions know of women who have followed the spiritual path and become women of wisdom, women empowered by the inner strength of the Spirit, which has enabled them to help and guide numerous other human beings, and to act as teachers, counsellors and guides. This is by no means only a phenomenon of the past – on the contrary there are numerous women guides and spiritual leaders known to us today although they only rarely possess institutional and administrative leadership positions. What is new, however, is our deeply transformed awareness of gender differences between women and men affecting all human experiences and activities, including the discovery, transformation and exercise of spiritual power. To recognize these differences more clearly and interpret their full meaning we need far more individual case studies and comparative analyses, such as are brought together in this book. The contributors give special attention to the experience of women as spiritual teachers or disciples in traditional religious contexts and also in new religious movements. Their papers deserve wide reading and discussion. At a time when many of our contemporaries are seeking new insights, counsel and guidance in an ever more perplexing world, attention to the powerful and inspiring examples of women experiencing all the strengths and perils of discipleship to the highest life of the Spirit may provide new models worth following for those seeking direction. At the very least others, less interested in the transformation of life, may still be challenged to consider these new perspectives worthy of critical intellectual debate.

Ursula King
University of Bristol

Acknowledgement

The editors wish to thank Valerie Lehmans for all her skill, hard work and patience in producing the camera-ready copy.

Thank you.

Introduction

'Women, Discipleship, and Spiritual Power' was the theme of a conference held at King's College London in December 1991. It took place at a time of growing interest in women's role in religion. In Britain the current focus is on the debate surrounding women's ordination, but this is symptomatic of wider changes in gender roles in society and the 'revisioning' of feminine values. The secular sphere has been transformed, through radical changes in male-female relationships and family life, and women's increasing participation in professional life. However, in the religious sphere progress has been somewhat slower – happening regardless, but not always recognized.

The last ten years have produced a growing body of research into women's role in religion – Western and Eastern, old and new. Much of the evidence points to a continuation of traditional, i.e. subservient roles for women: cleaning the temple rather than running it; numerically predominant as followers but rarely found in priestly or leadership roles. In some movements the issues are vigorously debated, challenge leading to change, but in others the status quo is maintained, supported by theology and praxis.

The influence of feminism is strong on American Buddhism, and in paganism throughout the world, but has hardly impinged on many other movements, particularly the more conservative Christian and Eastern-based groups. But even where the theology is liberal, as in some new religions and 'New Age' movements, the social organization may be depressingly sexist. The reasons for this lack of progress are partly historical, stemming from the initial rejection by the Women's Movement of religion *in toto* as irredeemably patriarchal. It is only recently that women have begun to reclaim or create forms of feminist spirituality both inside and outside the Judaeo-Christian tradition. The second reason, more specifically relevant to this collection, is the predominance of male charismatic leaders, often supported by hierarchical, patriarchal structures – and, sadly, reinforced by female devotion with its inherent vulnerability to exploitation.

Given these developments, it may well be asked what is the relevance of discipleship to modern women? It is a difficult concept for feminists, since it seems to encapsulate and endorse the most disempowering 'feminine' qualities, discouraging women from claiming spiritual authority. It may even seem retrogressive, and yet historically it has been a spiritual path open primarily to men. For example, we are informed that all Jesus's disciples and most of Buddha's were men, the women being marginal even if the scriptures sometimes allot them a central role. However, women have generally been disbarred from active participation, let alone priestly or leadership roles, being considered impure and pollutant. So there is a sense in which discipleship is a privilege to be claimed.

On the other hand, insofar as women are granted any spiritual qualities, these are generally seen in terms of traditional 'feminine' virtues such as devotion, receptivity, humility, self-effacement. These could be said to comprise a feminine model of spirituality, but they are also the virtues of the good disciple. It could therefore be hypothesized that discipleship is a feminine path, and that women make good disciples. But the question that follows is: is discipleship good for women?

Does discipleship imply a model of male authority and female submission, thus reinforcing and even exploiting traditional stereotypes? Or can discipleship as a spiritual path be fulfilling, liberating, and even empowering? In India it has always been believed that the greatest blessing in life is to find a master. In the West, on the other hand, we hear more of the dangers and excesses of charismatic authority.

The papers in this volume take for granted a broad feminist consensus, which does not need spelling out. However, the links between feminism and discipleship, and the spiritual and methodological implications, are more contentious and provoked lively debate in the conference. The scope of inquiry ranged from the broad question of whether women should be disciples at all to the nitty gritty of power, emotional and sexual abuse, the integration of spiritual praxis with everyday life. Questions included were whether men can understand women's issues at all, and should women's studies be a segregated area; the related issue of women's spirituality and whether women should opt for separate development as a temporary or permanent solution. Also hotly debated were the virtues of chastity as a condition of spiritual attainment versus motherhood and family life; whether the latter was a distraction or a valid alternative path – immanence versus transcendence.

The contributors represent a wide range of traditions and approaches: Western and Eastern, old and new, scholars and practitioners. Three of the contributors hold leadership roles in their religious tradition, one is a disciple but also an academic, one is an ex-disciple. All have some personal interest in and experience of the issues, and write with the authority of their own combination of theory and praxis.

Discipleship is not a state much associated with Christianity, which is ironic given the pre-eminence of the relationship between Jesus and his disciples in his lifetime. However, in the early centuries of Christianity there was a trend for ascetics to retreat to the desert for mystical contemplation. In time these 'desert fathers' attracted many disciples. What is less well known is that there were also a number of female ascetics, whom Averil Cameron calls 'desert mothers'. Owing to the misogynistic attitudes of the periods, their lives and teachings were rarely documented. However, Averil Cameron has disinterred a considerable body of evidence about these women, many of whom were high-born Roman matrons who gave up their social position to meditate in the desert. There are not many examples of women in leadership roles, but some formed religious communities and monasteries, usually headed by women. However, they could not become priests or bishops. Generally, women were viewed with a mixture of fear and fascination by male monks and priests, as objects of temptation. One of the most popular images of female sanctity in the folklore was the repentant prostitute, the most famous being Mary of Egypt. It sometimes seems that the only recognised female virtue was chastity, hence the only way women could overcome male hostility and gain respect was by becoming a paragon of purity.

Hinduism comprises some of the world's oldest, most sophisticated and diverse spiritual traditions, including a model of female empowerment in the Great Goddess. As Devi or Shakti she is worshipped throughout India, and contains an enormous range of archetypal qualities. Ursula King asks how this symbolism relates to the actual lives and social status of Indian women, and finds that Indian society has remained patriarchal. Women are perceived as more powerful than men and feared on account of their powers, but have therefore been firmly controlled by men. They have a role in popular religion, particularly the devotional *bhakti* strand, but little religious authority. The Great Indian Goddess therefore provides a rich but ambivalent resource for women, with particular potential for the new goddess-worshipping movements, leading to a new disclosure of both the immanence and transcendence of divine reality, and to a rediscovery of the sacredness of life. In India women have tended to follow *bhakti*, be devotees rather than gurus, although this pattern is now beginning to change, for example with the Brahma Kumaris. Further research might demonstrate how far women disciples and gurus draw inspiration from the Great Indian Goddess.

Sara Sviri describes the classical model of discipleship in eastern religion, through the example of Irina Tweedie who became a disciple to a Sufi teacher. This paper documents the gruelling training she underwent with him, involving numerous tests and hardships: financial deprivation, physical hardships, scorn and rejection. This is the traditional Sufi way – fire to burn the dross of the ego – but for a privileged Westerner it was hard. In Sufi doctrine the heart is a vessel that needs to be prepared, purified to receive the experience of the Divine. The process requires a teacher, who has two roles: a passive role as a mirror of the divine, and an active function of using his own energy to ignite the love energy in the disciple's heart. Through this fire one becomes 'featureless' (*fana*), a process similar to the Christian *via negativa* or the Buddhist path to *nirvana*. Tweedie's teacher instructed her to keep a diary of her experiences which would become an aid to others, evidence that such experiences are still possible today. This diary is a record of a psychological struggle between ego and non-self, the grinding down of the wilful ego, the suffering of body and mind for the sake of spiritual transformation. She herself passed the test of absolute surrender as a disciple, and has now set up as a teacher in London with her own students. She is thus an exemplar of both sides of the coin: discipleship and mastery.

Traditionally the master-disciple relationship happens on a small scale, one-to-one or within a small ashram, as with Irina Tweedie. However, some gurus, particularly this century, have gone on to found new religious movements. One example of this was Brahma Baba, the deceased leader who founded the Brahma Kumaris in India in the 1930s, a movement that has now spread all over the world. Sister Sudesh, the UK director of the Brahma Kumaris, describes one of the most striking and exceptional aspects of this movement: the high status given to women, initially by Brahma Baba, but most of the leaders are still women. Whereas normally such 'feminine' qualities as love, service, humility are used to keep women subservient, here they are seen as qualities of greatness of soul fitting women for leadership. At the same time the Brahma Kumaris believe that women need to balance these virtues with the more 'male' qualities of courage, determination, clear thinking and self-respect. This last quality in particular can only be gained by knowledge of the eternal self which is beyond gender – an important concept in spiritual practice. The Brahma Kumaris see this form of mould-breaking as a positive way of changing society. They emphasize the importance of studentship as against discipleship, and omit such traditional gestures of reverence as touching the feet of the guru. The emphasis is on the members being family, and Brahma Baba is revered as the father. Members may still live in families, but celibacy is a condition for deeper spiritual growth, even between husbands and wives.

We have taken the opportunity to include another paper on the Brahma Kumaris written two years earlier by Vieda Skultans. This presents a sociological overview of the movement, in contrast to the more devotional insider's perspective given by Sister Sudesh. In many ways the two views coincide, since esteem for feminine qualities and the concomitant predominance of women is the most striking feature about this movement, and is duly noted by both contributors. However, there is an interesting divergence in the interpretations given to this characteristic. For example, Vieda Skultans takes note of the subsequent role reversal: whereas women take on the 'higher' spiritual duties, including most of the teaching, men look after the practical aspects of life. This includes dealing with the outside world, but also menial chores such as shopping, cooking and construction. She also notes the suspicion and ridicule provoked in India by the emphasis on celibacy for women, in a culture where this state is traditionally reserved for male renunciates. Yet this is the precondition for the role reversal, freeing women from the burdens of maternal and domestic duties. However, Skultans reveals one qualification of women's superior spiritual status. Brahma Baba's teachings are now relayed through female mediums in a trance state; they are valued for this function, but their power is muted by becoming simply mouthpieces for a male spirit. There was at one time a similar device at work in the Rajneesh movement when its leader Osho used female mediums to convey not words but 'energy' to other disciples in 'energy darshans'.

Another new religious movement founded by an Indian guru is the Rajneesh movement. It is publicly perceived quite differently from the Brahma Kumaris, largely because of an exaggerated media focus on its sexual permissiveness, and more recently on the dissolution of its headquarters in America. However, on a deeper level the two movements have strong similarities, especially in their basis in meditation as the path of knowledge of the essential self beyond the socially conditioned ego. The Rajneesh movement also had a male leader, Osho, who believed in women's superior spiritual qualities and promoted them to leadership positions. However, unlike the Brahma Kumaris, the master-disciple relationship is central though less so since Osho's death. Osho was a charismatic guru who drew on the Indian *bhakti* tradition, and perceived women as particularly capable of attaining on this path – of allowing the ego to dissolve through love, trust, devotion. Men were perceived as more ambitious and competitive, aiming to become masters whereas women were content to remain disciples. This very surrender would ultimately lead to enlightenment. Yet paradoxically, in leadership positions women disciples developed their strength and power, to an extreme. Ursula King speculates on the Indian Goddess as role model; Rajneesh sannyasins became matriarchs in the Kali mould. Many of these disciples were ex-feminists, but they did not object to 'surrendering' to a man, largely because they saw him as 'beyond gender' thus also beyond sexism. These women found that through Osho's own integration of his 'male' and 'female' sides they could do the same, thus finding empowerment in the very act of surrender.

Buddhism is another religion that originated in India, and also has as its goal the annihilation of the ego or self. From India it spread all over Asia, and in the last 100 years has gained a growing following in the West. Zen, which developed in Japan from its Chinese origins, is the best known and most popular form, especially in America. In this paper Anne Bancroft describes how it is based in the master-disciple relationship. Although Zen has strong hierarchical and patriarchal tendencies, women can become ordained. In Japan numbers are small, but in the West they are growing, and in America comprise about half the practitioners and even a small number of teachers. As in Sufism, there is a rigorous discipline requiring trust from the student, but not blind trust. Misunderstanding of the nature of this trust makes disciples, particularly women, vulnerable to exploitation, and there are numerous examples of betrayal of trust through sexual misconduct and the abuse of power, just as there are in the more controversial new religious movements. Anne Bancroft is the only contributor to this volume to examine this most contentious aspect of female discipleship – and, even more contentiously, the unfortunate collusion of women in their own mistreatment. However, she also sees the problem in a positive light, as a challenge for the growing number of Buddhist women meditators to overcome the male-dominated, hierarchical power structure, especially as they become *roshis* in their own right. She also sees the growth of a lay movement as encouraging a move towards a more democratic social organization and the integration of spirituality with everyday life – a uniquely female contribution to immanent spirituality.

Moving from Zen to Afro-Brasilian religion or Candomblé, Peter Clarke explains how women in the most adverse circumstances became prominent as teachers and priestesses, particularly in the state of Bahia in north-eastern Brazil. Former slaves who were forced by oppressive laws to rear and educate their children almost single-handed – women of African descent in Brazil – worked and saved to buy their freedom, joined Catholic religious associations for black people where they acquired organizational and leadership skills, and in the face of opposition from Church and State recreated the institutional base – the terreiro – which enabled Afro-Brazilian religion to survive, develop and eventually gain constitutional recognition. Today the most widely respected and sought after Candomblé priests and teachers in Bahia are women.

All the foregoing papers describe examples of women who participate very effectively in their chosen religious path, some even holding leadership positions. But in all these movements the women defer and submit to a male spiritual authority at some level, whether to a living or dead master, or to the gods. Paganism appears to be the only extant religion where a female priestess or goddess is herself the ultimate authority. The final two papers in this collection examine aspects of women in paganism, though from quite different perspectives.

Cecilia Gatto-Trocchi's paper is a critical examination of four charismatic feminist leaders of Italian movements. One is the leader of an Islamic sect, one of an esoteric positive thinking movement, and two lead pagan goddess-worshipping movements. These have both set themselves up in opposition to the Christian church and its violent misogyny, presenting the Goddess as a life-affirmative, transformative alternative. Barbara appears to condemn Christianity entirely, whereas Elvira Giro subverts the tradition by reinterpreting the theology along more feminist lines: the Virgin Mary as the great Cosmic Mother, the Holy Ghost as feminine principle. Gatto-Trocchi is critical of the danger of these women leaders as charismatic authorities, particularly the extreme devotion and submission that Caroline demands, and the personality cult she encourages, although she does instruct her disciples to follow her teachings, rather than simply imitating her.

Vivianne Crowley is an ordained priestess in the pagan movement, and presents Paganism as a radical, positive and transformative path for women. Several religions, including Hinduism – as Ursula King demonstrates – have Goddesses, but Paganism seems to be the only contemporary movement where the divine feminine or Goddess is both authority and role model – for men as well as women. Crowley sees Paganism as particularly relevant and empowering for Christians, whose religion is so lacking in positive and adult images of female spirituality. She presents Paganism as a way of exploring the feminine mysteries and rejecting the social conditioning that binds women. It is generally approached from one of three perspectives: ecology, particularly 'deep' ecology with its emphasis on the earth as divine or Gaia; feminism, with its reclaiming of women's spirituality; and Wicca, with its roots in the eighteenth-century occult revival, including the rediscovery of the pagan goddess worship that was suppressed by the church. In practice all these strands are woven together to create a powerful female collectivity. However, this kind of power is different from patriarchal power, which emphasizes domination and destruction; it is rather an inner strength that individuals are encouraged to develop in collaboration with other group members. Men and women initiate each other, on equal terms. There are gods and goddesses, but the Goddess is pre-eminent. Women are seen as particularly suited to leadership roles; men may also hold positions of authority but only through coming into right relationship with the female. The emphasis for women is on empowerment rather than discipleship, encouraging women to discover their own divine femininity rather than submitting to a male priest or god. Paganism may thus provide a strong and radical alternative for women's guilt and low self-esteem inherited from millennia of religious misogyny.

Altogether this collection comprises a multi-faceted and challenging examination of the issues of women's role in religion, both as students and disciples, and increasingly in priestly and leadership positions. The picture is changing all the time, more and more rapidly, though progress is by no means universal. While some religions offer unprecedented opportunities for women to explore their spiritual potential, the fundamentalist backlash pushes them firmly back into an inferior and subordinate status. It is hard to see which trend predominates, but at least the widespread dissolution of social and religious power structures provides an open space for experiment and change. There are clearly no easy answers, as this compilation reveals. However, what emerges is the beginning of a consensus that women have the right and ability to reclaim their spiritual potential on an equal footing with men, and in doing so to enrich the pluralism of the contemporary religious scene with some novel and creative solutions.

Elizabeth Puttick and Peter B Clarke
King's College London

1

Desert Mothers: women ascetics in early Christian Egypt

AVERIL CAMERON

According to accounts which reach back to the late fourth and early fifth centuries A.D., the desert of Egypt at that time was full of female monasteries and Egypt itself the home of many women ascetics. At Oxyrhynchus in the Thebaid, for example, it is reported that there were twelve churches inside the town, and that the lay people were outnumbered by the monastics, of whom the local bishop had no less than 10,000 monks and 20,000 nuns under his jurisdiction (Ward & Russell 1980: V). At Antinoe, further up the Nile on the opposite bank, there were twelve convents, in addition to 1200 monks and anchorites living outside the town itself (Clarke 1928: 163, 165). There were also women's convents among the 2-300 associated with the Pachomian site of Tabennisi (ibid. 115), one of which had as many as 400 nuns in it.

Were we to take these early stories and travellers' tales literally, we would have to imagine the Egyptian desert in late antiquity as populated with hundreds of monastic buildings and thousands of individual men and women dedicated to the religious life. But even allowing for the exaggeration of religious enthusiasm on the part of the authors and compilers of this literature, both the male and the female religious are too well attested for us to doubt that they did indeed exist in very large numbers by this time.

One of these early writers was the bishop Palladius, who composed an account of visits to the ascetics and monastics of Egypt, Palestine, Syria and Asia Minor. Palladius frequently mentions holy women, in a way which shows that he took them completely for granted. A bishop himself in Bithynia, Palladius dedicated his work to a palace official in Constantinople called Lausu, who, he tells us, had asked for an account of the 'saints', both male and female, whom he had encountered on his journeyings. One of his chapters is devoted entirely to holy women – 'distinguished virgins and widows' – including several of high rank who had adopted the ascetic life or founded convents (Clarke 1918: 141-42). Many others refer without special comment to holy men and women, as though the latter are to be taken entirely for granted.

Many fewer women are mentioned by name in the stories of the lives and collections of sayings of the 'desert fathers' which circulated at this time and which became a popular form of literature in the Byzantine world. However, this is probably more the result of the milieux in which such stories were collected and circulated than a true reflection of their number. Certainly women feature largely in the stories of Syriac monasticism of the fifth and sixth centuries, and some of the most popular tales circulating in Greek, Syrian and other languages in the early Byzantine eastern Mediterranean world were of female saints – Mary of Egypt, Pelagia, Thaïs among them. Romanticized though these are, they also reflect a situation in which women as well as men were well represented, both in the monastic communities in Egypt and elsewhere and as individual ascetics or even anchorites. Women saints are often represented in Byzantine church decoration, and women's monasteries continued to be important throughout the Byzantine era, and are frequently mentioned in Byzantine literature. In view of the highly exclusive and misogynistic attitude adopted by male monastic foundations in the later Byzantine world, and maintained to this day on Mt. Athos and elsewhere, this prominence of women religious in the early period is rather striking.

Special monastic rules for women were in existence in the fourth century, and the *Life of Antony* (d. A.D. 356), the first major classic of hagiographical literature, records Antony as having placed his sister in a community of virgins. Many women already lived lives of religious retirement on a more informal basis, whether in their own homes or with a few others. Some among the well-to-do had turned their homes into regular monastic establishments. I shall return to a well-known example of this for illustrative purposes at the end of the paper, and there is much to say about all these possibilities. However, the 'desert mothers' of early Egyptian monasticism particularly deserve to be recorded in a volume on women's spirituality and discipleship, as do the many female visitors who apparently made the journey to visit the many monks and nuns, and they will provide my main focus.

The latter category included several women of the highest Roman aristocratic background, who would, of course, have been most easily able to afford to make such a tour. Palladius had been preceded on his journey to the famous monastic region of Nitria by one of these, Melania the Elder. She had taken with her a casket containing 300 pounds of silver intending to give it to the holy man Pambo, only to find that he refused all such gifts. When he died soon after, Melania prepared his body for burial and buried him, having received from him the gift of his only treasure, the last basket he had made with his own hands (Clarke 1918: 61-63). Melania stayed for six months on the mountain of Nitria and visited all the ascetics there, before going to Palestine to look after the Origenist monks who had been imprisoned there. Dressed as a slave, she was not recognized, and regularly took food to the prisoners until she was arrested herself, whereupon she did not hesitate to pull her rank on the unsuspecting governor and obtain a quick release. Next, she founded a monastery herself at Jerusalem and lived there in charge of fifty women religious for some 27 years (ibid. 148-9).

Melania had a granddaughter of the same name who was to become equally famous, and in whose company Palladius visited Egypt together with Silvania, another Christian woman from an important official family. Melania the Younger sent money to Dorotheus, a priest who ministered to the anchorites of Antinoe, and much larger sums to other parts of Egypt and the Thebaid, not to mention to churches elsewhere (ibid. 163,168). Turning to the example of Arsenius, one of the Egyptian ascetics who had himself held high rank before his withdrawal, we find him asking to be spared the visitation of a high-class Roman lady, and claiming that if he was not careful he would be inundated by visits from others like her (Russell 1975: 13-14).

As we have seen, some of these ladies made their visits in the company of well known male friends. Paula, for example, took her daughter with her to Egypt when she went there with St Jerome before settling in Bethlehem, as he had. Jerome's friend and later rival Rufinus was a travelling companion of the Elder Melania, who also influenced the famous ascetic writer Evagrius of Pontus to become a monk in Egypt. The authenticity of some of the travel accounts mentioned in the literature has been doubted, although on insufficient grounds (Ward & Russell 1980: 4ff). However, it is clear that there was a network of contacts in operation between religious in Egypt and communities and individuals in Palestine, especially Jerusalem, and that rich and well connected women like Melania played an influential role both in travelling themselves and in bringing other people together.

Not all the women visitors were so eminent, of course, nor did they all succeed in making their journeys. We read in the Greek *Historia Monachorum* of a tribune's wife who was very anxious to see the aged John of Lycopolis. The latter, however, kept refusing to see her, and in the end she had to be satisfied simply with an appearance by the old man in a dream. Instead of seeing the women themselves, John preferred to deal only with husbands. In one case, he was able to tell the husband of his wife's difficult delivery and near escape from death, while on another occasion he cured a senator's wife of her cataracts at long distance rather than see her in person (Ward & Russell 1980:1).

In these examples the women have become nameless, and this is also the case with the female heads of most of the women's monasteries that are mentioned. Those who are known by name from the monastic literature include Abba Sarah, who is said to have waged war for 13 years against the demon of fornication, and to have lived beside a river for 60 years without ever raising her eyes to look at it (Ward 1975:229-30). Sarah was visited by monks from Scetis, and by two old male anchorites. True to the preoccupation of this literature with matters of gender, which we shall observe again later, the story has Sarah say to her male visitors 'It is I who am a man, you who are women'. When the two old anchorites imagine that as a woman she is bound to feel proud that they have come to see her, she turns the tables on them, saying, 'According to nature I am a woman, but not according to my thoughts'. However, despite this emphasis on gender difference, it is notable that Sarah, a woman, is held to be affected by the same sexual temptations as male ascetics.

From another 'desert mother'. Amma Syncletica, many sayings are recorded on the general conduct of the religious life, rather than on gender-related questions, among them the observation that if his mind is crowded with thoughts, a solitary in the desert may be as little at peace as if he were living in a town (Ward 1975: 234). Like Syncletica, Amma Theodora warned of the dangers of *accidie,* and of the attacks of demons on monastics (Kraemer 1988: 123-4). There is no observable difference between the wise sayings attributed to these two women and those put into the mouths of their male counterparts. Moreover, Theodora has monks among her questioners and listeners: 'another of the old men questioned Amma Theodora saying, "At the resurrection of the dead, how shall we rise?" She said, "As pledge, example and as prototype we have him who died for us and is risen, Christ our God"'.

The colourful fifth-century abbot Shenoute of Atripe, leader of the White Monastery, is said to have had under his jurisdiction over 2000 monks and 1800 nuns. Tachom, recipient of a letter from him, was the head of a women's monastery apparently associated with the White Monastery, and is called 'mother' by him (Kraemer 1988: 125-6). Many other women's monasteries are recorded, even though we do not know their abbesses by name (Bowman 1986: 194 ff). The nuns at Tabennisi, for example, had the same rule as the men, whose monastery faced their convent across the river. When one of the sisters died, the nuns prepared her body for burial and the brothers then crossed the river by ferry and carried it back for burial in their cemetery. This was the only occasion when the monks visited the women's monastery, except for the priest and deacon who went there on Sundays to perform the regular services.

Sometimes a man might unwittingly approach the convent, in which case suspicion could arise in relation to the nuns, leading to a scandal, or to the calling in of the priest to deal with matters (Clarke 1918: 116-18). But equally, nuns of the same monastery could become famous for their sanctity, like the 'holy fool' described by Palladius, whom the aged anchorite Piteroun was allowed to visit by special dispensation. When the two met, each fell down and asked for a blessing from the other, and Piteroun said to the other sisters, '"She is mother of both me and you" – for thus they call the spiritual women – "and I pray to be found worthy of her in the day of judgement"' (ibid. 119-20). Respect and friendship could also exist within smaller groups, as with Ammonius, disciple of the famous Pambo of Nitria, who settled in the desert in a group of three brothers and sisters, 'the women living separately by themselves and the men by themselves, so as to have a sufficient distance between them' (ibid.:64).

The existence of many women religious is therefore clear from the monastic literature, even when as so often the positive indications about them are often overlaid by a thematic of male suspicion of women, as illustrated in the story of a certain Elias, described as 'a great friend of the virgins', for whom he built a large monastery on his own land, perhaps at Atripe, and therefore not far from the White Monastery of

Shenoute. Into this monastery he brought 'all the dispersed women ascetics' – amounting to 300. Unfortunately, the women quarrelled incessantly with each other, and Elias was obliged to stay with them in order to keep the peace. 'Being still young, for he was some thirty to forty years old, he was tempted by desire', and went out into the desert to try to overcome it, whereupon three angels appeared to him in a dream, promising to cure him if he swore an oath to return and look after the women. The 'cure' took the form, in the dream, of castration by one of the angels. Elias swore the oath to look after the women and returned to the monastery, 'correcting' the nuns for another 40 years from inside his own cell. Despite remaining there, he somehow managed to see male monks as well as the nuns of the convent, for he is said to have often assured the fathers that he no longer felt any desire, this being the 'gift of grace' which he was granted in exchange for his stewardship of the monastery (Clarke 1918: 109-10). However, his successor was less able to achieve such a level of detachment, and resorted to the more extreme expedient of shutting himself up in an upper room and viewing the women through a window which he could open and shut when necessary. According to the report, Dorotheus stayed in this upper storey, to which there was no ladder, for the rest of his life (ibid. 110).

Temptation, and the conquest of temptation, are ever-present themes in this literature. The presence of women in whatever guise evidently represented both a fascination and a problem to the male monks. In a classic story (on which see further below), Abba Serapion seized the opportunity of visiting a prostitute in her dwelling for the purpose of praying with her and converting her to the religious life. The woman was overcome, and asked his assistance in changing her life, so he took her to a women's monastery and entrusted her to the amma there, who gratified her request to be allowed to be enclosed for the rest of her life in a cell fed only on bread and water passed to her through the window together with pious work for her hands (Ward 1975: 226-7).

Several stories suggest that neither women nor men religious were immune to the sins of the flesh, like the tale of the nun seduced by a minstrel (Clarke 1918:175). But pious women might also earn men's respect by their very virtue, such as Piamoun, who lived at home with her mother, to whom an angel revealed an impending attack on her village by men from outside. When she told the village elders, they were too afraid to face the attackers themselves, and beseeched her to go and meet them instead. Understandably, perhaps, Piamoun refused. Nevertheless, her prayers were so successful even at long distance that the attackers became nailed to the spot while they were still three miles away from the village (Clarke 1918: 111-12).

However, beauty did not always lead to sin. The lovely Taor, though a nun of 30 years' standing, was still capable of attracting 'even the most steadfast', but was preserved from such danger by her chastity and modesty (ibid.165). Conversely, Amma Talis, the mother of the same monastery at Antinoe and a nun of 80 years' standing, was so beloved that the 60 young women in her charge did not even need to be locked in behind the monastery wall, but stayed inside of their own free will – an interesting hint of the more usual kind of monastic discipline. Another beautiful woman, if the account is to be believed, was Syncletica, an upper-class woman who lived as an anchorite in the desert east of Jerusalem and who concealed herself so successfully that she was taken for a eunuch monk. Fed by God for 28 years, she had retained her beauty, but when the narrator of the tale returned to find her again, she was nowhere to be seen (Flusin & Paramelle 1982).

With Syncletica we are clearly in the realms of hagiographic romance, a genre which flourished in the eastern Mediterranean before the Arab conquest. Themes of transformation, gender reversal and penitence pervade the many accounts of reformed prostitutes and female saints who disguised themselves as men, only to be revealed on their deathbed. One of the best known of the former group was Pelagia, an actress from Antioch, whose story circulated in Syriac and Greek, and found its way in Latin translation to the medieval West (Ward 1987:57ff). There was also Thaïs, a prostitute visited by Abba Paphnutius in a more elaborate version of the story about Abba Serapion to which I have already referred; again, this story was also translated into Latin (Ward 1987: 76-84). In this account, Thaïs, after being enclosed in her cell in the convent, was the subject of a vision experienced by Paul, the disciple of Antony, in which he saw a luxuriously draped bed guarded by three angels. The bed was for Thaïs, and indicated that she had been forgiven her sins. Despite her protests, Paphnutius took her out of her cell, and she lived for another 15 years in peace.

Yet another was Paesia, subject of one of the sayings of the desert fathers, which relates to an ascetic called John the Dwarf. Paesia had been a pious orphan girl, who used her wealth to open a hospice for the monks of Scetis. But in time her money ran out and she fell into prostitution, whereupon she was visited by John with a view to her rescue from this life of immorality. Paesia was overcome by remorse, and went with the monk into the desert. When they lay down to sleep, John saw a shining pathway leading down from heaven, and angels taking up the soul of Paesia. When he woke, she was dead (Ward 1987:77-8).

The classic of this genre is perhaps the well known story of Mary of Egypt, of which there are also several variants. Mary, another prostitute from Alexandria, journeyed to Jerusalem with some pilgrims, where she was brought to repent when she tried to enter the church of the Holy Sepulchre (Ward 1987: 27-56). Afterwards she went into the desert near the river Jordan and lived there as a recluse for 47 years, until she was found by a priest called Zossima, in time to be recognized by him as a woman and given a suitable burial.

This and the other versions of this story, like those of Thaïs and Pelagia, belong to a context in which the figure of Mary Magdalen was also developed into the image of a repentant prostitute turned anchorite (Ward 1987:1055). They were extremely popular in the early Byzantine east and the western Middle Ages alike, circulating in numerous versions of differing levels of elaboration. The gender tensions with which the written versions are permeated are of course quite obvious, and it is apparent that they must belong to the least realistic stratum of the monastic literature. No one would want to suggest that the Egyptian and Judaean deserts in the fifth to seventh centuries A.D. were inhabited by many such exotic repentant prostitutes, any more than that the desert fathers really spent so much time successfully converting such women. However, to dismiss these stories as total fiction would be equally wrong, besides failing to acknowledge their undoubted psychological power.

As Benedicta Ward points out in her modest but excellent study, there is a positive side to their presentation of gender relations as well as a negative one. Between the prostitute and the holy man – Pelagia and the bishop Nonnus, or Mary of Egypt and Zossima – there is the possibility of a new kind of love relation 'which is fulfilled, and in no way denied, by their choice of chastity and solitude' (Ward 1987:65), and which is told with delicacy and tact in the texts. It is not simply a matter of a male monk leading a fallen woman back to virtue, for in some versions at least the women themselves become the repositories of wisdom and the guides in turn of their male counterparts. Their role as models of repentance is an obvious way in which this should have been so, as in the case of the nun made pregnant by a minstrel, whose child died, and who devoted herself to such feats of repentance and good works that a priest heard the voice of God saying 'So-and-so has pleased me more in her penitence than in her virginity' (Clarke 1918:176).

Their positive role also took more concrete forms, as with the 'virgin' – that is the dedicated religious woman – of Alexandria, and incidentally another reputedly very beautiful woman, who is said to have taken in and sheltered Athanasius when he was being pursued for his orthodox beliefs. She hid him for six years, 'washing his feet herself and ministering to his bodily requirements and arranging for all his needs, borrowing books and bringing them to him' (ibid. 169-71). Palladius's next chapter refers to a similar case in Caesarea in Cappadocia, where a certain Juliana sheltered Origen from pagan persecution for two years, allowing him to use her own library, which was apparently extensive (ibid. 171).

Even from this very limited survey, a picture begins to emerge of an early Christian world in which women religious are extremely numerous. They do not, it is true, occupy the positions of priests or bishops, and women's monasteries are dependent on men for the essential liturgical services. While I have concentrated here on the more positive pointers in the monastic texts without dwelling on the frequent signs in them of hostility to women, it is easy to see that even the passages which I have cited are often expressive of a male-centred discourse, which was if anything to crystallize still more as time went on. The surviving material has many problems of interpretation inherent in it, and does not permit us to see how far a specifically women's monastic literature was developed in female contexts. Given the nature of our sources, it is extremely difficult here, as elsewhere, to disentangle the actual role played by women in early Christianity from the way in which they have been represented in the overwhelmingly male literature (see e.g. Kraemer 1992: chaps. 10,12).

It is sadly true that the desert mothers who feature beside the desert fathers in the surviving literature are few in number. Nevertheless, alongside the clear preoccupations in much of the literature which I have cited with sexuality and temptation, and the consequent tendence to view women with a mixture of fascination and fear, there are enough more neutral or passing references to ammas, to women's monasteries and even to individual religious women, to show how numerous they must have been. The collections of 'sayings' of the desert fathers took shape over a period, and continued to be copied and reshaped in monastic environments in the succeeding centuries. However, the milieu depicted in most of the literature I have cited relates to the fourth and fifth centuries, the period of the establishment of Egyptian monasticism, and the descriptions in Greek and Latin by Palladius and

Rufinus belong in a specific context of interest in asceticism by many highly placed Christians in Rome, Constantinople and elsewhere.

The 'desert mothers' mentioned in the literary sources often have Coptic names themselves, and are therefore likely to be of local origin. But within Egypt, Greek and Coptic were closely linked, and, as we have seen, the monastic settlements in Egypt were more cosmopolitan than this suggests; this must also have applied to the women's monasteries, even if to a lesser extent. Some women were able to travel, and did not hesitate to do so. We have encountered the two Melanias and others. The most intrepid was probably the Spanish nun Egeria, who embarked on a long journey to all the holy sites of the east in A.D. 384, writing a vivid travel diary as she went (Wilkinson 1971). We should not assume that all the women who retired to the religious life in Egypt were illiterate Coptic peasants, any more than were the monks themselves. Indeed, Evagrius of Pontos, one of the most famous and controversial of the male monastics who features among the desert fathers, and who had gone to Egypt after earlier stays in Constantinople and Jerusalem, was a close connection of the Elder Melania and the author of precepts for the proper goals and regulation of women's monastic communities (Elm 1991). Some of the desert fathers in the late fourth century, and, one has to presume, the desert mothers too, were deeply involved in the Origenist controversies of the time, in which Evagrius was a leader, and the literature naturally also reflects these preoccupations.

One has to be cautious in using such texts as direct evidence. Even so, the number of women monasteries with their women leaders is very evident. Nor are we dependent on texts alone: both archaeology and documentary papyri amply attest the growth of monastic communities in Egypt (Bowman 1986: chap.6). Nor did the style of monastic life remain static. Excavations at Kellia, for example, have demonstrated that significant developments took place in the succeeding period in the style of living adopted by the anchorites, and large numbers of inscriptions and graffiti in Coptic from the sixth to the eighth century show that monastic life there was still flourishing, and indeed that it enjoyed an increase in numbers after the Arab conquest of Egypt in A.D. 641, until it began to decline in the later eighth century. The pottery from the same French and Swiss excavations has shown that these monasteries were by no means isolated from the general economy and that they apparently used the same imports that are attested by ceramic evidence elsewhere. The Egyptian monasteries were thus a major feature of the settlement patterns and general economy of the region.

Trying to recapture women's spirituality in the centuries of early Christianity is, however, no easy matter even when texts are available (see e.g. Kraemer 1992: chaps.10 and 12). More often, the problem, also lies in the very uneven spread of the evidence, not to mention its paucity in many important areas. Thus in the present case, while scholars are divided about many features of interpretation and dating regarding the early development of monasticism in Egypt, the available literary evidence, supplemented by the evidence from papyri, has meant that it is this earlier phase that has received most attention (see Gould 1992). It is in this context that we hear most about the women religious who are of interest to this volume. Clearly there were many women in leadership roles in these early monasteries – but as we shall see, frustratingly, the direct evidence that we have for them contrasts both in quantity and in the amount of detail with what is available for some specific examples in other areas.

It is often the asides, or the passing references in the monastic literature that tell us most about the women religious, allowing tantalisingly brief glances at what was clearly an established feature of Christian life during this period. Nor was it by any means confined to Egypt, for while in this short paper I have concentrated on Egypt, with its wealth of evidence and rich tradition of ascetic life, Palladius, for example, refers frequently to women religious and holy women in other regions, notably Asia Minor. Other sources such as the sixth-century *Lives of the Eastern Saints* by John of Ephesus, who had been a monk himself at Amida and wrote his *Lives* in Syriac (Harvey 1990), have a great deal of information to offer about women's spirituality and leadership elsewhere, especially in Syria, where women seem also to have played a very central role, 'strong and wilful, impressive as leaders who gain the respect of male and female alike, and found in roles not normally open to women in their society' (Harvey 1981:41).

Another monastic writer, and a great traveller himself, was John Moschus, who wrote his *Spiritual Meadow* in the early seventh century, and many of whose stories concern the religious life of Palestine, another great centre of monasticism in this period. However, the other main literary source for Judaean monasticism, the several *Lives* by the sixth-century writer Cyril of Scythopolis, have little to tell us about a role for women (Hirschfeld 1992). While some of John Moschus's tales do concern women, their main geographical focus is somewhat different and they tell us less than the earlier literature about leadership roles (Harvey 1981:41-42).

The 'desert mothers' of Egypt and elsewhere in the eastern Mediterranean in the period up to and just after the Arab conquest are known to us to a very large extent through a male literature which, while preserving honourable traces of their activity and influence, and allowing us to see, even if only dimly, how numerous they must actually have been, has nevertheless obscured their actual spirituality by presenting them within an ideological framework of holiness (male) and temptation (female). It is not so much an overt attempt to control, for, as we have seen, a number of these women are in fact described in extremely admiring terms, and women's monasteries are mentioned throughout with great respect. Rather, there may be particular reasons for the prominence which women do achieve in the early stages of the development of the monastic literature, which happened to coincide with the period of activity of some very influential Christian women. Several of these, as we have seen, visited Egypt themselves and were part of the network of those interested in monasticism and asceticism in Egypt and Palestine, even to the extent of founding monasteries themselves, as Paula and the Elder Melania did on the Mount of Olives.

In dealing with the early centuries of Christianity, as with the ancient world in general, it is always a matter of where the available sources happen to focus. The same is true in the present case. The 'desert mothers' of Egypt are not very well attested in comparison with their male counterparts. But there is enough information to let us see that they are just one example of a phenomenon that was widespread in the Christian world of late antiquity, namely the existence of women as leaders of religious communities, and women regarded as spiritual leaders in their own right by reason of the wisdom which others perceived in them.

A striking and, in comparison with the Egyptian ammas, well-documented example in the later fourth century is Macrina, the sister of St Basil (author of a highly influential rule for monastic life) and St Gregory of Nyssa, who persuaded her widowed mother to convert the family estate in the Pontos into a women's religious community. The whole of this large family seems to have been devoted to the pursuit of the ascetic life, and it is her brother Gregory, himself a bishop and important ascetic author, who composed the hagiographic *Life* of his sister (Maraval 1971). He lets us see something of the prayer life of the community which she led, and mentions two of her female associates by name: Lampadion, a deaconess, and Vetiana, a widow of senatorial rank who had been living with the nuns. Even more interesting for the present purpose is the glimpse which he gives of the relationship between Macrina as spiritual leader and the women who had accepted her in this role, and who included former slaves and servants of this rich household. Macrina is presented throughout as their leader and teacher; they grieve for her death as for a family bereavement, while Macrina's prayer on her deathbed effectively lays out the aims and goals of their religious life, in terms of the soul's aspiration towards God.

This text, too, has many problems for those who want to take it as historical evidence for women's religious communities, in that it is the work of one of the major theologians of the period, who has certainly used it to express his own highly intellectualized conceptions of ascetic life. How far we can assume that the specific character of Macrina's role as represented here was repeated in the Egyptian women's monasteries is clearly questionable. Yet to judge from the evidence that we do have, the ammas who are recorded in the literature of Egyptian monasticism exercised a similar spiritual leadership. They differed only in not having a Gregory to write about them.

References

Alan Bowman (1986) *Egypt after the Pharaohs, 332 BC - AD 642. From Alexander to the Arab Conquest,* Berkeley and Los Angeles

Sebastian P Brock & Susan Ashbrook Harvey (1987) *Holy Women of the Syrian Orient,* Berkeley and Los Angeles

W K Lowther Clarke (tr.) (1928) *The Lansiac History of Palladius,* London

S Elm (1992) 'Evagrius Ponticus' *Sententiae ad virginem, Dumbarton Oaks Papers* 45: 97-120

B Flusin & J Paramelle (1982) 'De Syncletica in deserto Iordanis (BHG 1318w)', *Analecta Bollandiana* 100: 291-317

G Gould (1992) 'Early Egyptian monasticism and the church', *Monastic Studies* 1:1-10

Susan Ashbrook Harvey (1981) 'The politicisation of the Byzantine saint', in S. Hackel, (ed.), *The Byzantine Saint,* London, 37-42

Susan Ashbrook Harvey (1990) *Asceticism and Society in Crisis, John of Ephesus and the Lives of the Eastern Saints,* Berkeley and Los Angeles

Y Hirschfeld (1992) *The Judaean Desert Monasteries in the Byzantine Period,* New Haven

Ross Shepard Kraemer (ed.) (1988) *Meanads, martyrs, matrons, monastics. A Sourcebook on Women's Religions in the Greco-Roman World,* Philadelphia

24

Ross Shepard Kraemer (1992) *Her Share of the Blessings. Women's Religions among Pagans, Jews and Christians in the Greco-Roman World,* Oxford

P Maraval (1971) *Grégoire de Nysse. Vie de Sainte Macrine,* Sources chrétiennes 178, Paris

Benedicta Ward (1987) *Harlots of the Desert,* Oxford

Benedicta Ward & Norman Russell (1980) *The Lives of the Desert Fathers,* Oxford

Benedicta Ward (1975) *The Sayings of the Desert Fathers,* London and Oxford

J Wilkinson (1971) *Egerias Travels,* London

2

The Great Indian Goddess:
A source of empowerment for women?

URSULA KING

In their rediscovery of the attraction and power of the Goddess, contemporary feminists make selective use of ancient religious traditions and frequently draw on prehistoric and early historical data. Some gain particular inspiration from the Goddess figures of the Ancient Near East, Greece, Rome and Egypt, others look at contemporary examples of living Goddess worship. There are perhaps few places on earth where Goddess worship is as much alive as in India but, apart from a few exceptions, the feminist Goddess and Wicca movement has so far drawn little on this rich tradition, perhaps because it is not sufficiently well known in the West.

For most Western women it is perhaps less a question of constructing an alternative tradition of Goddess worship than of exploring complementary symbols and images which modify and enrich the traditional God image of the Judaeo-Christian tradition. Here the significance of the Great Indian Goddess can be a tremendous resource and inspiration for 'revisioning' our image of the Divine and for providing a source of empowerment for contemporary women.

Divine female symbolism in Hinduism

All our images and concepts of the Divine must be recognized as human constructs which can be helpful as 'doors of perception'. Yet they turn into prison walls if we do not recognize their limitations and acknowledge the need to look through other windows too. Looking at the Divine through an Indian window opens up some extraordinary perspectives, for few languages possess the richness of classical Sanskrit and other Indian languages, and few cultures have produced such a wealth of symbols to express and point to the multiform manifestations of divine life. Not only are there representations in human and animal form, but there also exist personal and transpersonal manifestations and understandings of the Divine, especially in the way the Indian tradition has reflected on *Brahman* as Ultimate Ground and Reality. From the perspective of women it is particularly attractive to discover how much Divine Reality is imaged in Hinduism in both female and male forms, and how very diverse and significant the female symbolism for the Divine is, not only in general terms, but how it dominates and takes priority over any other among certain Hindu worshippers.

Scholars have acknowledged that Hinduism presents the most developed example of feminine dimensions of the sacred in the contemporary world. Female images of the deity are as numerous, popular and well developed as those of male deities. Goddesses in countless forms are portrayed in worship either alone or with their husband consorts, as 'spouse goddesses'.

Hinduism is a highly literary tradition dominated and closely controlled by the power of male Brahman priests who have handed down the sacred Sanskrit texts of Vedic literature and its many commentaries since ancient times. There are few references to Goddesses in the Vedic texts, but at the popular level of Hindu worship there have been many Goddesses whose origin may go back to the Indus Valley civilization. Small figurines have been found from the ancient Mohenjo Daro civilization of the second millennium BCE which represent the Great Mother or Nature Goddess, and some ancient Indian texts allude to the existence of a mother of all created beings, sometimes perceived as 'mother earth' or later as 'Great Mother'. Goddess worship dominates much of modern Hindu village religion and may always have been important at village level, whereas male deities have dominated much of the Hindu textual tradition. The texts on the Goddesses developed much later. During the early medieval period (about 600 CE) several fierce Goddesses, often active on the battlefield, became widely known in Hinduism. It is often said that the three great Gods of Hinduism are Brahma, Vishnu and Shiva, and thus the most important Goddesses are their consorts Sarasvati, Lakshmi and Parvati. In fact, if Hinduism is seen as a family of related religions rather than one religion, it is clear that Hindu worshippers are largely divided between devotees of Vishnu, Shiva and the *Devi* - the Goddess.

Some of the strongest feminine imagery in religions is found at the level of folk religion where it is almost universally present and where the Divine is often perceived and worshipped as mother. This very ancient tradition relates to a basic human experience that carries a rich symbolism, though it is not without ambiguity, as I have discussed elsewhere (King 1989b). In India, especially in the south, the village Goddesses are seen as 'village mothers' (*matas*) who possess both benevolent and malevolent powers and have to be appeased in various ways. Furthermore, there is also a belief in India that water is benign and life-giving and therefore rivers are sacred and imbued with motherly qualities. Reverence is given above all to 'Mother Ganges', represented as a female Goddess figure. Indeed, the whole of India is revered as sacred, as 'Mother India', and understood to be identical with the power of the Goddess.

Most revealing and puzzling are the different Goddess figures who complement and to some extent even contradict each other in their activities and nature, as described in their mythological stories. The Goddess is either portrayed and worshipped alone as *Devi* ('Goddess') or as spouse Goddess, as consort to a male deity. The relationship between Indian Gods and Goddesses is a complex one and can be understood in three ways: first, the male God is dominant and the Goddess is subordinate to him; second, both are equal as can sometimes be seen in the relationship between Radha and Krishna or also in the androgynous form of Shiva, the Shiva Ardhanarishvara. In the third type of relationship the Goddess is dominant and the male God subordinate to her. There is not only ambivalence in the Goddess theology depending on whether she is seen as spouse Goddess subordinated to a male God or as independent Goddess, but there is also further tension between malevolent and benevolent aspects of the Goddess - the Goddess both protects and needs to be appeased so that her wrath and harmful powers are kept at bay. There are many local and regional Goddesses, but they are often identified with one or the other of the great Goddesses known all over India. Some of the most important ones are Sarasvati, Lakshmi, Parvati, Kali and Durga. I cannot describe these here but shall speak of the Great Indian Goddess, the *Mahadevi*.

The Great Indian Goddess

In Hinduism there is a theological assumption that all the many Goddesses are manifestations of one unifying cosmic principle known by many names, but characterized as active, powerful, and female. This great being is called the 'Goddess' (*Devi*), 'Great Goddess' (*Mahadevi*), and also *Shakti*, meaning power and energy, which suggests that inexhaustible creative powers are associated with this great Being. India also knows a kind of female 'trinity' consisting of *Mahakali*, *Mahalakshmi* and *Mahasarasvati*, but this is less well known than the male *trimurti*.

In India the divine feminine can be seen in varying and highly nuanced relationships to the divine masculine – as consort, lover, mother, sister – but it is also celebrated as an Absolute in supreme independence. The glorification of the Great Goddess is celebrated in the *Devi-mahatmya* ('The Exaltation of the Goddess'), a text which dates from around the sixth century CE and forms part of the daily liturgy in Indian Durga temples. It was translated into English as early as 1823, and is thus one of the earliest religious texts from Hinduism to become available in the West, but Western scholars have only recently shown an interest in studying its affirmations.

The *Devi-mahatmya* affirms that there is but one true ultimate reality, and that it is feminine. This reality takes on different forms which the ignorant mistake for separate existences, but the wise recognize as grounded in the *Devi*. The Great Goddess, the *Mahadevi*, is related to male deities, as to all that exists, not through an external relationship as consort, but internally, as their very power or *shakti*, the very energy through which all Gods act. The text establishes the primacy of the *Devi* in a cosmic context: she is the supreme ruler of all earthly creatures and the entire universe; she is victorious over all adverse powers. The *Devi* is celebrated for her salvific activity, for she possesses the knowledge which sets one free. But she is also the great illusion that keeps one bound, for she is equated with *maya* (illusion) and *prakriti*, primordial matter from which all else evolves, which through her becomes divine. Matter is no longer seen as the material shroud veiling the spirit, but as itself supremely divine, as the *Devi* herself.

The *Mahadevi* has many names. She is called root of the world, she who transcends the universe, she who has no equal, she who pervades all, who is the support of all, the ruler of the world, who is omnipresent. She is also primordial matter – *Mulaprakriti* – and the *Mahamaya*. But this identification gives a positive dimension to both *prakriti* and *maya*, for the emphasis is not so much on the binding aspect of matter as on the *Devi* as the ground of all beings: the central point here is that the *Devi* is the world, she is all creation; she is one with her creatures and creation. Both reality *and* illusion are subject to her.

The *Devi* is known in innumerable shapes and forms, both auspicious and terrible. She gives protection and fertility, grants wisdom, learning and liberation, embodies female beauty and desire, is the source of food and nourishment, and in one of her forms – the *Gurumurti* – she is the Guru, the teacher who bestows knowledge. As Stella Kramrisch has written about the *Devi*:

> She exists eternally, embodied as the world. She is Mahamaya, the great illusion, the great magic spectacle. She performs it with a purpose, and it is for this that she draws into herself all her forms, all her powers. She displays them, spends them inexhaustibly, overwhelms and thus binds man to her so that he may possess them in her beauty – and be free, liberated from his fascination, from his bondage to the world, to Maya. Mahamaya is Consciousness herself. Even more than that she is Mahavidya, transcending knowledge ... the great dormant power ...
>
> The Great Goddess takes everything within herself by her ultimate power, that of Consciousness (Kramrisch 1974:264)

The power of *Mahadevi* or *Shakti* is sometimes toned down by being 'spousified', closely associated with Shiva in particular, but the independent power and energy of the *Devi* is particularly celebrated in Tantrism which places priority on the female rather than the male principle, and where harmony and balance rest in the female principle in union with the male. The different Tantric schools have developed a complex set of rituals which cannot be discussed here, but some lines from a hymn may be quoted which express the greatness of the *Devi*:

> That Power who is defined as Consciousness in all beings, reverence to Her, reverence to Her, reverence to Her, reverence.
>
> That Power who is known as Reason in all beings, reverence to Her, reverence to Her, reverence to Her, reverence, reverence.
>
> That Power who exists in all beings as Shadow, reverence to Her (etc.)
>
> That Power who exists in all beings as Energy, reverence to Her (etc.)
>
> That Power who exists in all beings in the form of Species, reverence to Her (etc.)
>
> That Power who exists in all beings as Peace, reverence to Her (etc.)
>
> That Power who exists in all beings as Loveliness, reverence to Her (etc.)
>
> That Power who exists in all beings as Compassion, reverence to Her (etc.)

That Power who exists in all beings in the form of Illusion, reverence to Her (etc.)
That Power who exists in all beings as Mother, reverence to Her (etc.)
(Mookherjee & Khanna 1977:181-3)

The *Devi* is also invoked as World-Mother (*Jagadamba*) who helps and protects her devotees by freeing them from all anguish. The worship of the Divine Mother has been developed to its fullest extent by the *Shaktas* whose worship is associated with many well known temples in India. The mother image is perhaps more primal and basic than the notion of the metaphysical One who is the Goddess; grounded in universal human experience, Goddess worship is often an expression of the attempt to return to a primary bond of origin. The motherhood of the *Devi* has universal and cosmic dimensions, for the *Mahadevi* is called the root of the world who pervades the whole universe and transcends it. She is sometimes described as 'knowledge-of-the-Immensity' and as 'the Resplendent One', but one must not forget her ambivalence, for she possesses innumerable auspicious and also terrible forms.

The image and status of Indian women

Given the rich female symbolism of the Divine and the challenge of the metaphysical idea of the *Mahadevi*, the one great exalted Goddess, ruler of the universe and creative source of all that exists, how does this important belief and symbol relate to the actual lives of Indian women, their image and status in Indian society? Here we have to admit a great hiatus, for Indian society has remained male-dominated, and both female and male deities have supported the status quo. It is sometimes pointed out that Indian men are more involved with Goddess worship than the women are. Indian women have not been liberated socially and politically by the symbol of the Great Goddess – nor have women elsewhere – and yet Indian women also find great empowerment through *shakti*.

In its general sense *shakti* means the power or energy of the universe, understood as a female generative force, fundamental to all action. *Shakti* is thus both power and action, and both are female. The generative power of *shakti* appears in the power of the earth, its power of endurance, generation and transformation. *Shakti* is also the power of the Gods, the energy through which they act, for it is said: 'Shiva without *shakti* is a corpse'. In a more specific sense this all-pervading energy is itself divinized, in the form of the Great Goddess as *Shakti*. Within Her all powers come together and are unified, whether they are the powers of procreation, development or destruction; the powers of enjoyment, perfection, knowledge or sacrifice; or the powers of cruelty, time and death. She is the supreme point of the coincidence of all opposites where all contradictions are finally resolved.

In India women are perceived as innately more powerful, because they are *shakti*-filled. In South India it is said that man has the strength of an ant whilst woman has the strength of an elephant. Thus we have the contradictory situation that women are thought to inherently possess more power than men, yet remain subordinate to men who control them. If female powers are properly controlled, they are a source of protection, strength and blessing; if unchecked, they create havoc and destruction. Through their *shakti* women provide an essential link with the Divine; they are more explicitly identified with it and provide a focal point for the relationship between humans, the Divine and the cosmos.

Given this powerful vision and insight, what is the reality of women's power? Does the attractive and inspiring idea of *shakti* confirm the power of women, or does it perhaps mask the real situation where women have no power at all? How does the traditional image and status of Indian women relate to the power of the Great Goddess?

In India, as elsewhere, women's status remains closely linked to traditional religious ideas. However, Hindu belief is wide-ranging and includes many contradictions, and Hindu practices vary widely according to specific religious groups, particularly in different castes and regions. There is in particular a marked difference in the status of women between the north where Islam has had an influence over many centuries, and the south where different cultural traditions have been prominent. Because of these many regional and caste differences, my remarks are only valid in a general sense.

If we examine Hindu beliefs, most often quoted are the words of the ancient *Laws of Manu* where, in opposition to the powerful Goddess, we have the image of the subordinate, controlled wife: 'In childhood a woman must be subject to her father, in youth to her husband, and when her lord is dead, to her sons. A woman must never be independent.' The traditional duties of a woman, her *stridharma*, are those of wife and mother, roles which are greatly idealized. The ideal wife is faithful and uncomplaining; her virtue lies in the services she renders to her husband, a belief expressed through many stories of Hindu mythology. There is a contradiction here, too, for traditional role models focus almost exclusively on Hindu women as wives, rather than mothers, whereas at the divine level the image of the Goddess as Mother Goddess (which implies independence) ranks higher than that of the Goddess as divine consort or wife (which implies subordination).

Theologically, women are ranked on the same level as low castes or outcastes, for traditionally they are not allowed to study the Vedas or perform any sacrifices. According to textually sanctioned Hinduism, women have little religious authority, but in popular religious practice women have important roles, especially in the devotional or *bhakti* strands of Hinduism. Women are responsible for the all-important family worship and take an active part in many rituals connected with life-cycle rites and festivals, especially rituals essential for the well-being of their husband and children. At the village level we find women exorcists and shamans who manifest the power of the Goddess by becoming possessed by her. Women also celebrate several fasts, vows and rites of their own, which give them affirmation, strength and empowerment.

It is generally agreed that Indian women enjoyed a higher status in ancient times, especially during the Vedic period, than in subsequent centuries. However that may be, Hinduism is not unlike other world religions in that it possesses a double typology of women expressing either their equivalence with or subordination to men. First of all, at the ultimate philosophical level no sexual opposites exist in the One that is *Brahman*. Then a positive affirmation of the beauty, strength and power of women is found in the concepts of *shakti* and the *Devi*. Yet her figure is ambivalent, too, as she is associated with both benevolence and malevolence. Finally, at the social level attitudes to women may range from glorification to negation; the status accorded may vary from one of equality and power to that of unjustifiable subservience. This sense of ambivalence also relates to women's traditional roles: as mother a woman is more venerable than a teacher or father, and as such she is idealized and even deified by men, whereas as wife a woman does not have equal status with her husband. Motherhood always enhances a woman's status, especially when a male child is born. For religious and social reasons female children are seen as much less desirable. (Contrary to the relationship between female and male mortality rates worldwide, India has a higher female than male mortality rate for every age group.)

In connection with marriage and motherhood many religious rites are celebrated. For example, Gujarati women celebrate an annual fast (*Jaya Parvati*

Vrat) in honour of Shiva and his wife Parvati for the welfare and longevity of their husbands, whereas unmarried girls fast annually in honour of Parvati in the hope that she will give them a good husband. During a woman's first pregnancy a rite is celebrated known as 'inviting the *Mata* (literally the Mother Goddess). This can also be performed on other occasions whenever the help of the Goddess is sought, but the rite must include the honouring of *goyani*, of unmarried women or married women whose husbands are alive, who are considered sisters of the *Mata*, but are essentially treated as if they were the Goddess, whose creative power and energy are celebrated. Sometimes very young girls are worshipped during a night vigil as incarnation of the Mother Goddess, a rite which is still regularly celebrated among Gujaratis in Britain. Yet how is such exaltation, such 'deification' and praise of woman to be reconciled with the traditional expectation that the same girls will fit into the confining structure of traditional Indian family life in a British urban setting? Many women suffer here under the strain of two very different cultural norms, and in some cities in Britain special refuge houses for Asian women have been founded.

To return to women in India: there are growing reports of dowry deaths of young Indian women; there is occasional news about an illegal 'suttee' – the burning of a woman on her husband's funeral pyre; there is the 'devadasi' problem in the South where young girls, especially from untouchable castes, are dedicated to the temple service of a Goddess and in practice finish up in prostitution; and there are complaints from professional Indian women that they possess no Hindu role models to inspire and confirm them as women in their own right. Protest about women's subordination and exploitation is expressed in the contemporary literature of young Indian women writers and poets and in the feminist magazine *Manushi*. Much work towards changing the situation of women has been done over the years by different social reformers and Indian women's organizations, including the Joint Women's Programme of the Christian Institute for the Study of Religion and Society (CISRS, Bangalore and New Delhi). Yet so much more remains to be done. Given the complex and very uneven social situation of Indian women in the Indian subcontinent and many countries abroad, what meaning and significance has the Great Indian Goddess for our Indian sisters and us today? How far can the Great Indian Goddess be a source of empowerment?

The meaning of the Great Goddess for women

The Hindu tradition provides exuberantly rich, but also very ambivalent, symbolic resources for contemporary women. Religious ideas about women's power and subordination coexist but, as in Christianity, ideas about women's subordination have prevailed in practice and provided the dominant model. However, even in a position of social subordination traditional Indian village women have been able to draw strength from *shakti*, the power of the Goddess, and through their special rites have felt empowered by Her. At the same time educated and urban Hindu women can draw a new pride and strength from the rich female symbolism of their religious and cultural heritage.

If *shakti* is the power to do, is action, it can be experienced as natural, physical, mental, psychic and spiritual energy; it can be *jiva shakti*, 'soul power' or 'life power'. There is also an Indian belief that women possess great spiritual power acquired through suffering, especially the suffering of servitude. This gives women a moral superiority, a power which is creative and unifying, not destructive. Thus woman is regarded as the power that holds the family together, but there is also a belief in an essential, unbreakable unity among females themselves. Thus *shakti* is a power of solidarity, of the strength gathered through gathering together, a process of unification and an experience of solidarity among women that transcends cultural boundaries. As an American woman anthropologist has commented: 'This I believe is the central significance of the doctrine that the goddess *sakti* has many names and many forms and lives in many places, and yet she is still *the* goddess: one goddess, one power, one *sakti*. Her power consists in this union of many.' (Egnor 1980:27)

Can the Great Indian Goddess be a source of empowerment for women outside India? In terms of historical origin one cannot prove that Goddesses, whether in India or elsewhere, reflect women's own religious experience, or that they are projections of the minds of men. Yet the rich historical symbolism of Goddess imagery can provide significant resources for contemporary women seeking wholeness, affirmation and strength. The American scholar Rita Gross (1978) has argued that Hindu female deities present a much neglected resource for the contemporary rediscovery and reimagining of the Goddess. In terms of the composite image of the Indian Goddess she sees as of particular value the polarity of the Divine (as divine couple or in androgynous form), the strength, beauty, transcendence and dynamic creativity of the Goddess (especially as Durga), the coincidence of opposites, the emphasis placed on God as Mother, the association of important cultural activities with the Goddess (Sarasvati and Lakshmi), as well as the emphasis on her sexuality which helps to overcome the body-spirit dichotomy and positively correlates sexuality and spirituality.

Since religious symbols reflect as well as organize and shape cultural and social worlds, one can ask whether Indian symbols can be used selectively. For example, can some of the dark and abhorrent sides of the Goddess (which I have not discussed here) be left out of consideration altogether, and can the positive features of the Goddess be made significant outside their original religious context? Larry Shinn has argued at length in a challenging article on 'The Goddess: Theological Sign or Religious Symbol?' that whilst one might have recourse to ideas about the Goddess for theological reflection, she cannot become a powerful religious symbol for devotion and worship in another culture. He questions the assumption of most feminist Goddess theologies 'that the gender of religious symbols *necessarily* has a homologous or one-to-one relationship to the psychological, social and religious self-understandings of men and women' (Shinn 1980:179). I think this is a legitimate objection which needs to be taken seriously. He also writes:

> What makes the historian of religion uneasy with selective reconstructions of symbolic imagery taken out of historical context such as Gross offers ... in the Indian Magna Mater, is that all of the attributes named ... are obvious and well-known in a variety of goddess contexts *except* how they may liberate women socially and politically. The historical record of the goddess symbol is exactly the opposite ... (In) a male-dominated Indian society ... both male and female deities support the status quo socially and politically ... to 'reimage' a Goddess *for* women should cause one to question whether the theological enterprise is the place to start rectifying injustices for women. (Shinn 1980:197, n.35)

I would argue, against this, that the transformation of the social order goes hand in hand with a revision and sometimes even a reversal of the symbolic order. The two are interactive and influence each other. We fully acknowledge the ambiguity of the Great Indian Goddess with her dark and bright sides; we clearly recognize that the Great Goddess, tremendous source of energy and powerful focus of Hindu worship that she is, has nonetheless not given Indian women the social power, equality and dignity that is their due. In spite of these legitimate criticisms we must also perceive the tremendous challenge that the Great Goddess represents as idea, symbol and religious reality. We must take up this challenge and ask ourselves how she can validate and empower us as women and how, in reflecting on our female and feminist experience in relation to her, she can be a source of deep theological insight that can lead to a new disclosure of both the immanence and the transcendence of Divine Reality.

In principle I agree with the contention that we need universal, inclusive symbols for the Divine which ultimately transcend gender symbolism. An exclusive Goddess image for women alone is no real theological solution, but as the image of God in the Judaeo-Christian tradition has been so often conceived as a single transcendent male divinity, I can perceive much justification, harmony and balance for expressing what is universal through the female mode where metaphors for God are drawn from female rather than male experience, for a change.

The Great Goddess is universal and experienced as such by both her female and male devotees. Given our current social and political problems, the Goddess possesses many inclusive characteristics besides female ones which could help to heal the wounds of our world. She is not only the Mother of the universe, fervently worshipped as *Amba* or *Ambika* by Gujaratis, but she is the stream of life, the sacred power of nature, earth and cosmos which can make us rediscover the sacredness of all living things. She is also the power of unification who can draw all human beings together, the energy that unites and purifies, and as one of the incarnations of *Lakshmi*, she is *Shanti*, the Goddess of peace whose power we are so greatly in need of. The Great Goddess has many meanings – some are particularly empowering and attractive for women whilst others are fully inclusive and universal. All theology concerned with a fuller exploration of Divine Life and Being and its relationship to the whole of creation should take into account both dimensions.

Although outside the scope of the present essay, it should also be mentioned that, as far as I know, Hindu – Christian dialogue has so far not concerned itself with exploring the many theological dimensions of the Great Goddess. This is an important area for fruitful further exploration. An additional resource and inspiration for women, besides the Great Goddess, is found in the many outstanding Hindu women saints and mystics.

Traditionally women have been followers of *bhakti*, the way of devotion, whereas the way of renunciation (*jnana*) was closed to them. They could follow a guru but not be a guru themselves. However, in modern Hinduism there has been a marked change in this pattern in that more women now seek empowerment as ascetics on the *path* of *jnana* and act as gurus in their own right, (Denton 1991; King 1984). One of the best known examples of this was Ananda Maya, but there are many others and they usually attract both female and male disciples.

It would be of considerable interest to investigate in detail how far contemporary Hindu women gurus and disciples draw their inspiration and spiritual power from the worship of the Great Indian Goddess. Perhaps someone would like to take this up as a future topic of research – it is certainly a subject of considerable importance and powerful attraction.

References

C Mackenzie Brown (1990), *The Triumph of the Goddess*. The Canonical Models and Theological Visions of the Devi-Bhagavata Purana, Albany:State University of New York Press

Carol P Christ (1987), Why Women Need the Goddess, in *Laughter of Aphrodite, Reflections on a Journey to the Goddess*, San Francisco: Harper & Row, pp 117-32

Thomas B Coburn (1984), Consort of None, Sakti of All: The Vision of the Devi-mahatmyya, in J S Hawley and D M Wulff, *op cit*, pp 153-65

Lynn Teskey Denton (1991), Varieties of Female Asceticism, in Julia Leslie (ed), *Roles and Rituals for Hindu Women,* London: Pinter Publishers, pp 211-31

Margaret Egnor (1980), On the Meaning of Sakti to Women in Tamil Nadu, in Susan S Wadley, *op cit* pp 1-34

Rita M Gross (1978), Hindu Female Deities as a Resource for the Contemporary Rediscovery of the Goddess, *Journal of the American Academy of Religion,* XLVI/3, pp 269-91

J S Hawley & D M Wulff (eds), (1984), *The Divine Consort: Radha and the Goddesses of India,* Delhi:Motilal Banarsidass

Pupul Jayakar (1990), *The Earth Mother: Legends, Ritual, Arts, and Goddesses of India,* San Francisco: Harper & Row

Ursula King (1984), The Effects of Social Change on Religious Self-Understanding: Women Ascetics in Modern Hinduism, in K Ballhatchet and D Taylor, (eds), *Changing South Asia: Religion and Society,* Hong Kong: Asian Research Service, pp 69-83

Ursula King (1989a), *Women and Spirituality: Voices of Protest and Promise*, London: Macmillan

Ursula King (1989b), The Divine as Mother, *Concilium,* December, pp 128-37

David R Kinsley (1975), *The Sword and the Flute, Kali and Krsna: Dark Visions of the Terrible and the Sublime in Hindu Mythology,* Berkeley: University of California Press

38

David R Kinsley (1986), *Hindu Goddesses: Visions of the Divine Feminine in the Hindu Religious Tradition,* Berkeley: University of California Press

David R Kinsley (1989), *The Goddesses' Mirror: Visions of the Divine from East and West,* Albany: State University of New York Press

Stella Kramrisch (1974), The Indian Great Goddess, *History of Religions,* 14 (1), 235-65

Ajit Mookherjee (1988), *Kali, the Feminine Force,* London: Thames & Hudson

Ajit Mookherjee & Madhu Khanna (1977), *The Tantric Way: Art, Science, Ritual,* London: Thames & Hudson

Ralph W Nicholas (1982), The Village Mother in Bengal, in J J Preston, (ed), *Mother Worship: Theme and Variation,* Chapel Hill: The University of North Carolina Press, pp 192-209

C Olson (ed), (1983), *The Book of the Goddess: An Introduction to Her Religion,* New York: Crossroad

James J Preston (1987), Goddess Worship: Theoretical Perspectives, in M Eliade (ed), *The Encyclopedia of Religion,* vol 6, pp 53-8, New York: Macmillan Publishing Company; London: Collier Macmillan Publishers

Larry D Shinn (1980), The Goddess: Theological Sign or Religious Symbol?, *Numen,* 30, 176-98

Susan S, Wadley (ed), (1980), *The Powers of Tamil Women,* Foreign and Comparative Studies/South Asian Series, no 6, Syracuse University: Maxwell School of Citizenship and Public Affairs

3

Women as spiritual leaders in the Brahma Kumaris

SISTER SUDESH

In a world where women have been seen traditionally as someone else's wife, mother, daughter, or sister, why would a woman choose to follow a spiritual path? Perhaps because deep inside, every woman has a longing to 'be' someone in her own right – fully aware of herself, confident and in control. When we talk of spiritual power, we are referring to the original power of the self to be whole and independent – free from the web of domination and suppression, free from the need to exist for someone else's sake.

For the last two thousand years or more women have not fully utilized their spiritual power. Instead, aspects of the 'feminine' have taken merely stereotyped symbolic forms, from the Virgin Mary to the vestal virgins, from Earth Goddesses to the shakti Devis. On the one hand, women have been put on pedestals and worshipped on account of their purity or femininity. On the other hand, they have been excluded from religious practices, and are still barred from entering some places of worship.

Elevated or chastised, exonerated or condemned, the main problem facing women is that they have never been treated as equals to men – either as spiritual leaders or spiritual seekers. This lack of equality has its roots not only in sociological and cultural systems, but also, more particularly, within levels of consciousness, upon which spirituality is ultimately based.

Women as spiritual leaders

Women become spiritual leaders when they themselves acknowledge that they have the capacity and attributes to play such a role. The change of consciousness needed is to move away from unworthy feelings and attitudes and to see the greatness contained within the self. Feminine qualities such as love, tolerance, compassion, understanding and humility are also qualities of leadership. They are needed for spiritual progress, for without them it would be impossible to come close to God and attain self-realization. Every human being possesses these qualities, but women are more easily and naturally able to tap them. In any religious gathering it is usual to find more women than men. Feelings of love and devotion are often more natural to women, combined with a profound sense of discipline and order. A true leader leads through example.

Women know how to serve and how to give. Often the notion of service or of putting others first has been seen as a sign of weakness or lack of power. Quite the opposite is true. The ability to bow before others, with true humility, is the sign of the greatness of a soul who has conquered ego.

However, this quality of giving to others must also be balanced with qualities of courage, determination, clear thinking and self-respect. Too often women have a tendency to give to others and neglect their own spiritual needs. It is one of the major reasons women find themselves depleted and lacking in spiritual power. The foundation for assuming spiritual leadership is thus an enormous change of consciousness. Overcoming the physical, religious and sociological barriers that have prevented women from becoming spiritual leaders can only be done through the development of self-respect. The quality of self-respect comes from the knowledge and experience of the eternal self, which is beyond social, cultural or sexual identity. The eternal self or soul is pure, peaceful, and complete with divine and spiritual qualities. When women touch this inner, eternal core, they gain the courage to play the part they are capable of.

Spiritual power is an expression of the inherent qualities of the spirit and has nothing to do with gender or physical limitations. Freedom from the fear of domination or oppression occurs when there is awareness of superiority or inferiority. Feelings of equality, however, manifest when there is consciousness of spirit or soul. These feelings and attitudes can be expressed in actions, with positive results.

A change of consciousness is the starting point, but change does not end here. Women are still a long way from enjoying positions of spiritual leadership, and society still does not fully concur with the notion that women make good spiritual leaders. But society won't necessarily change until someone, whether an individual or a group of individuals, breaks the tradition and sets a new role model. This, at least, was the thinking behind the work of Brahma Baba, founder of the Brahma Kumaris World Spiritual University.

The historical context of the Brahma Kumaris

In 1936, at the age of 60, Dada Lekhraj, a wealthy diamond merchant from the province of Sind (now Pakistan) was overcome by a series of powerful visions. He had always been religiously minded and had also held a highly respected position in the community. But the visions changed his life completely, revealing striking images of the world passing through a period of immense unrest, as well as images of the changes required to usher in a new world for the future. Within a year or so, Dada Lekhraj, later known as Brahma Baba, had sold his business and established a spiritual university. He nominated a group of 12 young women to assume all administrative responsibilities for the group of almost 400 people which now met together regularly to study the knowledge given by God.

At that time in India women were treated as second-class citizens, perceived as little more than chattels belonging to their husbands. Such attitudes have their roots in the traditional Hindu scriptures. For example, in the Ramayan, there is a reference to four things being equal:

A drum (that you beat)
An animal (that you push)
A senseless fool
A woman

The Jagat Guru (World Guru) Shankaracharya, founder of the path of sannyas (renunciation), about 1500 years ago called women 'the doorway to hell' or 'a serpent'. In the efforts of the males to renounce vices and in particular to become celibate, this image of women helped to justify many men leaving their wives and children destitute while they went off in search of spiritual progress. Even recent poetry in India describes women as 'the heel of a man's left foot'.

At the same time there are references to the reverence of women within Hinduism: 'Where women are worshipped, there is the temple of the deities'. The main objects of worship are also the Goddesses: Saraswati, the Goddess of Wisdom; Durga, the Goddess of Power; Lakshmi, the Goddess of Wealth; Santoshima, the Goddess of Contentment; Seetla, the Goddess of Coolness.

For Brahma Baba to place women in charge of a spiritual university at a time when they were still hidden by the veil – literally and figuratively – caused a huge uproar. But Brahma Baba was determined to carry out this gentle social and spiritual 'revolution'. He believed that the balance of spiritual and social power would not change unless the inequalities were addressed, and women, both young girls and mothers, were given the right to serve the world as spiritual teachers. 'God has put the urn of knowledge on the head of the mothers', Brahma Baba would often say when encouraging and inspiring women to play this new and unfamiliar role.

By the time Baba Baba passed away in 1969, the knowledge he had been given and the changes he had championed had found receptive and fertile soil. Within the space of 54 years the University has grown considerably and now operates 1800 centres in more than 55 countries – 44 of them in Britain. All the administrative and spiritual duties are carried out by Dadi Prakashmani and Dadi Janki – two senior women teachers who have been students since the University's foundation.

Studentship not discipleship

Today, from an organizational perspective, both men and women assume responsibility for teaching and running centres. However, acknowledged policy is that men follow Brahma Baba's lead and willingly put the women 'in front'.

For the Brahma Kumaris (literal meaning: daughters of Brahma) the concept of discipleship does not exist. The closest words to that concept in the Hindi language are *chela* – the one who practises something (usually loosely translated as 'follower') and *shishya* – the one who studies.

Brahma Baba never positioned himself as a guru. He taught through example, by putting into practice the knowledge he had been given by God, and he encouraged others to do the same. For example, the touching of feet, and special personal services – which often accompany traditional master-discipleship relationships in India – are simply not entertained at the University. The relationship is one of a spiritual family with the father (Brahma) accepting the wisdom of the children with love.

Instead each one considers her/himself to be a student studying to become a master of the self through a change of consciousness. Brahma Baba encouraged women to understand and explore their hidden potential and inspired them with a vision of how much contribution women can make as spiritual leaders. He found that women have the serenity and gentleness to understand and accept spiritual ideas easily without the barrier of arrogance that is so often present in men. However, by placing women in front, to redress the situation of imbalance within our societies, Brahma Baba sought to create a situation of equality and mutual respect and regard between men and women, and indeed within all relationships regardless of gender. At the Headquarters of the University in India, it is mostly men who are responsible for the running of the 42 departments and many men are teachers and administrators.

Thus neither sex is subservient to the other and there is greater harmony and unity in all relationships. With the spiritual training and spiritual authority there is a recognition of the specialities and strengths in others which is the basis for unity. What allows such spiritual authority to develop is that for students of the Brahma Kumaris the focus in meditation is God, not any human being or physical image. There is therefore no suppression of the mind by anyone, but the mind is free to be creative, alert and clear. The kind of education that Brahma Baba was offering was not, therefore, a blind devotion but an education that was accepted with understanding, something that both the head and the heart could agree upon. It is an attitude of constant learning that enables people to work with humility and self-respect.

Even now, though Dadi Prakashmani and Dadi Janki (both in their 70s) have 54 years' experience of teaching meditation and helping others to develop their spirituality, they still consider themselves to be students. Within the University the quality of humility is considered to be one of the greatest spiritual qualities. It is this quality that has enabled both these women leaders to travel the world, offering advice and spiritual educational to world leaders, groups of professionals and people generally.

Spiritual training is offered at two levels; firstly through silent meditation and daily morning spiritual discourse containing the teaching of the Raja Yoga. This is attended by teachers and students alike, whether they have 54 years' experience or 4 weeks. Secondly, lectures and classes are delivered by senior teachers based on their understanding of the practice of meditation and Raja Yoga teachings and disciplines in today's ever-changing world.

The aim is for each student to use the knowledge received and the experience given in meditation to lead a happy and purposeful life, whilst at the same time working towards the attainment of self-mastery and a loving relationship with God. Thus the University functions as a place where students discover for themselves their own innate qualities and abilities. In turn they use them for the benefit of society and world change. Through harnessing their spiritual power, students, both men and women, develop essential leadership skills. They then employ these skills voluntarily within the community, offering courses in meditation, self-development, confidence-building, stress management, within a wide community-based arena including schools, hospitals, youth clubs, homes for the elderly, prisons and businesses. On an international level, the Brahma Kumaris World Spiritual University organizes international peace conferences at its mountain headquarters in Mount Abu, Rajasthan, India, as well as seminars and workshops for professionals relating to the development of a better world.

In this way there is a transference of personal and social skills across the board, all offered on a voluntary basis. In recognition of its work internationally the University became affiliated to the Department of Information of the United Nations as a non-governmental organization in 1980 and later received consultative status with the Economic and Social Council and UNICEF.

Spiritual power and transformation

Members of the University share a clear vision of the future. It is a world in which men and women, regardless of race or colour, play an equal role through the harnessing of their own spiritual power. This can only happen when the energy of the soul is expressed through a proper balance of male and female qualities. The qualities of love or compassion alone can be rendered ineffective in some situations unless they are balanced with discipline and detachment. Spiritual power means using accurate resources at the right time and in the right way to effect positive change on the outer level. Yoga, which literally means union, is about developing a loving link with God in order to remove weaknesses and bring into balance the male/female qualities of the soul. Raja means sovereign and when added to yoga indicates that human beings attain mastery over themselves, their energy, consciousness, and inner qualities – when there is a strong connection with God.

Raja Yoga as taught by the Brahma Kumaris is about world transformation on the basis of self-transformation. Women play an important part in this process. This is because their style of spiritual leadership not only ensures a redressing of the balance of power in society, but also provides a nurturing environment in which all members of the human race can progress.

4

The Brahma Kumaris and the role of women

VIEDA SKULTANS

During the past twenty years new religious movements have multiplied and there has been a parallel growth in the literature documenting their development (see, for example, Barker 1982). Many of these movements have come from the East and from India in particular. Whether they are truly 'Indian' is a matter of some debate. The argument has been conducted both in terms of their congruence with the ideas of classical Hinduism and in terms of demonstrating intellectual roots within a Western religious tradition, despite a terminology which might lead one to suppose otherwise (Oden 1982). In both cases there is a danger that this kind of approach may obscure important features of the new Indian religions, particularly as they are practised in India.

This paper, therefore, aims to redress the balance of discussion in that it deals with the Brahma Kumari movement in India, rather than its exportation to England and the West.[1] It does not deal with theology but with social relations within the movement. This approach yields an interesting view of the roles assigned to men and women within the movement. Whereas there is a considerable body of work which demonstrates how women are controlled by men and assigned an inferior status,[2] this is without doubt a movement where women control men. Women occupy positions of power and status, whereas men, both in their secular and religious roles are subordinate to women. This subordination of men to women depends upon an inversion of family structure and a reversal of sex roles. Furthermore, the maintenance of this role reversal rests upon the practice of celibacy.

My first contact with the Brahma Kumaris took place in February 1981. They invited me to give a paper at their international conference in Delhi. It was they, not I, who perceived the relevance of my earlier work on Welsh Spiritualists to their activities. My two weeks in Delhi and at their headquarters in Mount Abu, Rajasthan, convinced me that here was a fruitful field of study, so in the summer I set off for a three month pilot study visiting centres in the north and south of India.

The movement was started in 1937 in Hyderabad by a Sind diamond merchant who had made his fortune in Calcutta. It was a largely Moslem community in which Hindus were represented by two rival castes, the Baibunds and the Amils. Membership of the new movement was drawn from the Baibunds who were merchants and less educated than the Amils who were civil servants. The first intimations of a new religious development came when Dadi Lekhraj began to receive visions and auditory messages, which grew to become the Brahma Kumari religious knowledge and practice. He had always been of a religious disposition and a pious Hindu, but in his sixtieth year he began to receive divine visions of a startling nature, in particular visions depicting the destruction of the world.

The movement has a precise beginning: during a *satsang* held by a *sannyasi*, Dadi Lekhraj, who had always been renowned for his courtesy, walked out of the assembly and withdrew to his room. Thereafter, he began to attract a following of women to whom he revealed the nature of his divine visions and messages. Neighbours and relatives began to flock to Dadi Lekhraj's house in order to be able to follow the religious way of life more perfectly.

Although Baba, as he came to be known, did not purposefully train women, they naturally came to the forefront. Baba thought that women were intrinsically of a more spiritual nature and more trustworthy. Nevertheless, there were men in the movement from the start, and they dealt with practical matters. However, the movement has always been feared by men and many of the men who joined initially backed out later. In particular, men were afraid that family feeling would be destroyed and, indeed, they were right in this respect. Also, there was much initial hostility from the families of members. Wealthy and influential men created animosity through the newspapers and rumours were spread of immoral sexual behaviour. A number of much publicized lawsuits were set in motion against the institution by irate husbands whose wives had fled from their marital and domestic commitments. Thus the suspicion with which new religious movements are generally received was exacerbated by the fact that the movement was drawing women away from their families. This general antagonism eventually precipitated a move away from Hyderabad to Karachi in 1938. Here a trust of fourteen women was set up to look after the finances of the movement. One original member of this trust, Didi, is now elder sister at Mount Abu. Another early member has acted as secretary for the movement and recorded Baba's sermons in shorthand. Many women fled from their families with no clothes or money and had to be provided for and protected.

After partition in 1947, families became concerned for the safety of their religious relatives and agitated for them to come to India. In 1950, therefore, the Brahma Kumaris left Karachi. In all, 275 people moved, travelling by ship and then by train to Abu Road. This initial period until 1950 is described by the Brahma Kumaris as 'going indoors' or 'going underground'. The thirteen years of quiet interior life were seen as a necessary consolidation and preparation for the more active proselytizing which is now taking place. It was a time of visions and ecstatic experience, when importance was attached to devotion rather than learning. In fact, the features of the Brahma Kumari doctrinal edifice were only very dimly perceived at the beginning. Now, by contrast, the details of spiritual knowledge are very precisely formulated.[3]

Particularly since Baba's death in 1969, the movement has expanded westwards as predicted. The real expansion of the movement occurred after the opening of the first centre in Neasden, England, in October 1971. It followed the wave of Indian immigration to England during the 1960s and the burgeoning of the new religions during the same period. In this way the movement could also draw upon the social openings and absence of restrictions enjoyed by women in the West. The movement is not concerned with charitable works of any kind. According to Roy Wallis' classification it could be described as world-rejecting (Wallis 1978). There are, it is claimed, about 80,000 Brahma Kumaris. Most of them are scattered throughout India, but several thousand are to be found in the West (and other more exotic parts of the world), such as the West Indies and South America. However, these figures may be an overestimate because the Brahma Kumaris are anxious to emphasize their growth and to remove any hint of their marginality. However, although there are about 500 centres throughout India, numbers are relatively small. Centres house between one and twelve full-time members, and classes vary between two or three and thirty or forty. There are about 100 brothers and sisters at the headquarters in Mount Abu, Rajasthan. There are many other sub-centres in which one room is set aside as a meditation room within an ordinary family house. Thus a picture emerges of relatively elaborate administrative arrangements to cater for the religious needs of comparatively few.

The Brahma Kumaris see themselves as primarily a women's movement. Indeed, the very name implies this: Kumari means unmarried woman in Hindi; Kumar means unmarried man. However, there are a large number of men within the movement. The founder himself was a man and it is argued that his masculinity was essential at the start of the movement for it to be taken seriously. However, most of those who are full-time members of the movement, who have dedicated their lives or 'surrendered', are women. Of the 1000 dedicated members, about 900 are women. However, men play a very important, if not always acknowledged, part in the movement. For example, sisters in all the centres which I visited depended upon brothers for dealings with the outside world. Such dealings concern everyday menial chores such as shopping for food, or problems arising to do with rent or purchase of the centres or providing furnishing. In such matters the sisters confess themselves not only helpless but also unwilling to devote time which they feel they could more profitably spend on spiritual matters. The organization of exhibitions and religious fairs is also the responsibility of brothers, although the decisions to organize these are made by women. Men look after the practical aspects of living thus freeing women for higher spiritual duties. This division of labour according to sex is partly a concession to general social norms in India – for example, respectable women tend not to shop in rural parts of India – and partly to the different religious roles allocated to the sexes.

Although the Brahma Kumaris are in the dualist tradition and sexual differences are thought to be unimportant in the sense that the body is seen as clothing for the soul and one might equally well be wearing a different garment, at another level the qualities of femininity give women the religious edge over men. However, there exists a certain ambiguity in this respect which is never fully resolved. If masculinity is a mere accident of birth then this should not in principle debar men from the pursuit of spiritual perfection. In practice, however, it does appear to be a hindrance. For example, women are thought to be more sensitive, tolerant, patient, gentle and above all spiritual. Feminine attributes are closer to divine attributes. This makes them better teachers than men and puts them into closer contact with spiritual reality. Therefore, it is usually women who give instruction in spiritual knowledge and meditation and who are the final arbiters on mystical matters. In adopting this position the Brahma Kumaris depart radically from traditional Indian beliefs and attitudes: feminine attributes may be revered as divine when they are embodied in a goddess, but certainly not in a mere woman. Men, by contrast, are thought to possess greater practical competence in dealing with the physical and social world.

When I questioned the Brahma Kumaris about brothers at the various centres, I was told that brothers did not live in the centre. When I disputed this claim and said 'What about brothers x, y and z?' I was invariably told that they were exceptions. In other words, men are an actual but unacknowledged presence in the movement. As far as classes are concerned, well over half the pupils are men and the male pupil and female mentor is a typical combination. In most anthropological monographs women are presented as a muted group, but in the case of the Brahma Kumaris the victims are men. However, what struck me most forcibly was that the relationship between the brothers and sisters living permanently together in the centres most closely resembles a family. Strict celibacy, of course, distinguishes the religious household from an ordinary household, but the uninformed might be forgiven for overlooking the difference. Apart from their rigid timetable and early rising at 3.30 a.m. the centres frequently consist of a jolly and intimate household of several women and one or two men with occasionally a child living in the centre. The men participate in the religious activities of the day but they also go out to work and do the shopping. However, men also help with the cooking and certainly with the washing up. Bedtime is the occasion for friendly chatting, laughter and a review of the days activities. It seems a trifle ironic that a movement which puts a very awkward spoke in family life by insisting upon celibacy within marriage should then reproduce so convincingly the outward form of married life. However, men appear to be playing the role of wives whereas women are clearly the spiritual and moral leaders.

At Mount Abu there are roughly equal numbers of men and women and in this instance the male presence is openly recognized. The Brahma Kumaris claim that Mount Abu is in fact the only place where brothers are allowed to live in. Be that as it may, the male contingent is particularly important in the running of daily activities and in the present construction work which is going on. Men work in the kitchens and it is acknowledged that much of the work involving the lifting of heavy pans would be too arduous for women. Interestingly, however, the main kitchen is run by a woman. However, the kitchen in which food is prepared for the older sisters is run by a young man. For the past year construction work has been going on for the building of a new meditation hall. This has involved excavating part of a rocky mountainside, all of which has to be done by hand. The supervision of this work as well as some of the physical work is done by the men. The dirtiest jobs, such as sweeping and cleaning lavatories, are carried out by servants who are local tribes people. At Mount Abu the women tend to be elderly and, therefore, less physically active. Younger women are distributed in the different centres throughout India. The young men are, therefore, essential for carrying out the tasks which the ageing Kumaris can no longer perform.

Women's most important role is that of teacher, but although women are acknowledged to have an easy and intuitive grasp of spiritual knowledge, the actual content of the classes is dictated by the *murlis* which are read word for word by whichever sister happens to be in charge of the class. The original *murlis* were sermons delivered by Baba and taken down by his secretary. However, after his death he returned through the mediumship of Sister G, then a young and unlettered girl who has since been the mouthpiece for hundreds of posthumous *murlis*. The interesting point to note is that although women play such an important part in the movement and although their qualities are so highly valued, nevertheless their power is veiled, in this instance, through the device of possession. Women, even when they possess power, cannot be seen to wield it. Hence, the importance of spirit possession where women are the instruments or mouthpieces of a male spirit.

The movement is not short of money and this too appears to accrue to the movement through its female members. A large number of Brahma Kumaris have apparently written over their personal wealth to the movement, or donated their earnings to it. In the case of young Indian sisters who dedicate themselves to the movement, the movement receives what would in the ordinary course of events have been a dowry. Since sisters tend to be recruited from relatively prosperous castes, the dowries tend to be correspondingly large. For example, the Brahma Kumaris have just acquired a third property in London, namely, a house in Chiswick. This was given as a kind of dowry by the father of one of the Indian sisters now living in London.

She is now in her early thirties and her father, who is not altogether sympathetic to the movement, has clearly abandoned hope that his daughter may change her lifestyle and decide to marry. The financial advantages accruing to the movement in this way are reminiscent of the enrichment process of medieval convents. The Brahma Kumaris themselves point to their austere lifestyle in explanation of their wealth. Unlike the rest of society, they do not spend money on cigarettes, alcohol or such frivolous pursuits as cinema-going or social entertaining. In addition it should be said that the Brahma Kumaris are astute housekeepers and managers of money.

The characteristic which sets the Brahma Kumaris most apart from ordinary life is celibacy. The movements preoccupation with purity is exemplified in dietary restrictions and in the demand for absolute celibacy for all, i.e. both within and without marriage. Sexual activity of any kind is equated with lasciviousness and lustfulness and described as a vicious habit. Again, Brahma Kumaris deny that celibacy has a detrimental effect on marriage, and indeed argue that it enhances the quality of marriage by creating greater mutual respect. Be that as it may, this stipulation of total celibacy surely puts the Brahma Kumaris in a unique category. A number of the Brahma Kumaris have indulged in 'vicious habits' before their introduction to the movement and have even had children, but after conversion celibacy is apparently total and unwavering. In a number of cases whole families have become converted and therefore live separate and celibate lives.

This demand for total celibacy for all has resulted in the movement being viewed in India with a certain amount of suspicion and even ridicule. Although the spiritual advantages of celibacy are widely recognized and particularly so in India, the fact that celibates are women and frequently married women excites some alarm in the mind of the average Indian. Celibacy is seen as being appropriate at certain stages of the life cycle, particularly the later ones, and for certain special categories, but as a universal prescription which ignores social and domestic position it is unheard of.[4] However, the Brahma Kumaris are adamant that their followers whilst showing complete commitment to the movement are nevertheless able to carry out their domestic and social obligations. Indeed, they contrast their position with that of certain *sannyasis* who go off into the wild after a family quarrel and abandon all earthly commitments.

Whatever the differences of opinion may be regarding the Brahma Kumaris' fulfilment of their domestic and marital duties, it is clear that the principle of celibacy plays an important role in the movement. Celibacy has been widely recognized as conferring spiritual power and social advantage. For the Brahma Kumaris celibacy is a precondition for achieving the role reversal necessary for the spiritual development of women. Complete abstinence enables a break to be made between the earlier social and domestic roles of women and their new religious roles: without it the old norms governing relations between the sexes would be carried over into the new spiritual life. Celibacy opens up the possibility of more varied relationships with men, of female dominance and also of a kind of camaraderie which would otherwise be unthinkable.

Yet another feature of the Brahma Kumari movement which is related to the dominant role of women is the presence of a small but highly significant Western minority. The majority of members are non-English-speaking *vaisyas*. Some of the elder sisters have become Westernized, but this is largely through the international activities of the movement. However, the two leaders of the movement speak hardly any English despite coming from very wealthy families, and I had the impression that their lack of language enhanced rather than detracted from their charismatic position. Their typical way of communicating spiritual power was by fixing their gaze and thus giving blessing. Apart from several dozen highly articulate and Westernized Brahma Kumaris, the vast number have had little contact with the West. The Brahma Kumaris themselves say that the native Indian understanding of the doctrinal niceties of the movement is limited. However, they are thought to excel in their devotional capacity. Westerners, by contrast, are thought to be particularly quick and penetrating in their perception and understanding of doctrine. They are often told that although they are the last, they are the first, i.e. although they are chronologically the last to join the movement they are first in their understanding of it.

The Westerners are mostly young professionals and students, with slightly more men than women. Certainly Westerners are assigned far more importance than mere numbers would warrant. Accommodation has been built with Western visitors in mind and food is adapted to suit Western palates. Lavatories are certainly built with Westerners in mind. To a certain extent such behaviour is part of being a gracious host, but it is not entirely explained as the result of politeness. Western centres receive far more visits from senior Brahma Kumaris than their tiny number would warrant. This suggests that Westerners and Western approval are indispensable to the movement. Naipaul has written that the interest of the West has always been important to India, even or perhaps especially in spiritual matters. The expansion westward was predicted by the founder of the movement as taking place after his death, so that subsequent events have, in fact, confirmed his prophetic powers. In fact, more contact with Westerners was necessary for the survival of the movement after its reallocation of power to women.

A large number of writers have documented the decline of women's position within Hinduism and Buddhism (see, for example, Altekar 1938; Dube 1963; Leslie 1983; Rudra 1975). However, the religious position of Indian women is not one of simple powerlessness. All the Hindu gods have female consorts so that the female principle is well represented among the Hindu deities. In each case the goddess has several aspects, some sinister and destructive, others benign and domesticated. Lawrence Babb has argued very persuasively that the transformation from sinister to benign depends upon the relationship of the goddess to her consort (1975: 223). 'When female dominates male the pair is sinister, when male dominates female the pair is benign' (226). Writing about the temples in Madhya Pradesh, Babb says: 'When they (Shiva and Parvati) are pictured together in lithography, Parvati again is standing beside her consort in a submissive attitude. But when the goddess stands in her terrible aspect in a temple, there is no god beside her' (223). Unlike the Christian tradition which accords the female principle a secondary place, in the Hindu tradition female deities enjoy an openly acknowledged, albeit subordinate position in the spiritual hierarchy. From the purely religious perspective the scope for women's participation in religion would appear to be greater in India than in the Christian West. However, the social obstacles to and prejudices against an independent women's religious movement would appear to militate against the development of a fully-fledged Hindu women's movement.

The birth and growth of the Brahma Kumaris testifies to the movement's ability to draw concurrently upon ancient Hindu traditions and the benefits of Western social influences, and to blend them in such a way as to overcome the disadvantages of each culture considered on its own. By this I mean that they locate themselves within the Hindu tradition which accords spiritual power and prestige to women and at the same time profit from the liberties and opportunities accorded to women in the West.

Hindu scriptures deny women independent ritual status on account of the polluting qualities of menstruation and childbirth and, perhaps, of female sexuality as such. As a consequence women have not been able to participate fully in Hindu religious life; their religious activities have been confined to the home. Thus the Brahma Kumaris represent a radical departure from the traditions of Hinduism.

Roy Wallis has questioned the future of religion in its sectarian manifestations. He writes:

> Religion in its newest guises finds itself isolated in tiny sectarian enclaves of believers alienated from and at the periphery of the industrial economy, or appealing to a broader constituency only by the massive attenuation of traditional form and content. Religion has withdrawn to the fringes or into privacy. The gods have been reborn but in such isolation or such reduced circumstances can they long survive? (1978:30).

The growth of the Brahma Kumaris testifies not to an attenuation of religious life but to a religious resourcefulness which draws upon both Hindu beliefs and Western practices. The suspicions attendant upon women practising an independent religious life in India are partly rebuffed by the protection which Western contacts afford. On the other hand, Hinduism offers greater potential spiritual rewards for women. For example, all devotees are conceived as being female in relation to Brahma. The combination of the two traditions affords a unique possibility for spiritual and social advancement. Perhaps, also, the strength of the movement derives from the fact that religious sects in India have played a different role from their Christian counterparts.

Ann Charlotte Eschermann in an unpublished paper (presented at a conference in Sri Lanka on 'Religion and Development in Asian Societies' in 1973) analyses the reasons for the inappropriateness of transferring the Christian concept of a sect to an Indian context. In the Christian tradition the term 'sect' has negative connotations, designating schools of thought which are not only different but also wrong. Christian sects have traditionally been opposed to 'church' and have reinterpreted established traditions. Unlike the equivalent English term which implies heterodoxy, the Hindi term *sampradaya* means orthodoxy. As Eschermann writes:

> What does constitute a Hindi sect is not the fact of being rejected by a central authoritative institution. It is the tradition founded by a 'sage' a 'saint' (*acarya, guru*).

Her paper points to the danger so aptly described by Clifford Geertz of assuming that if we create pigeon holes we will find the same pigeons in them and, indeed, any pigeons at all (1968:23-4). In India the sects have played a major part in the modernisation or radicalisation of society the – *Brahmo Samaj* is an example (see, for example, Kopf 1979). Thus the Brahma Kumari movement has created a highly innovative and adventurous role for women, which appears to be deliberately chosen in preference to alternative styles of life.

William James in his chapter on conversion cites the proverb which claims that man's extremity is God's opportunity (1960 edition:213). Although this may have applied to the early conversions where women escaped from tyrannical husbands, it appears to be no longer the case. In most cases conversion takes place as an orderly event in the life cycle. The typical pattern is for women to finish their education, very frequently to a high level, and then to dedicate themselves to the movement as an alternative to a worldly career or marriage. Dedicated brothers tend to keep their outside employment even when they are living in the centres. Sometimes they retire early in order to be able to devote themselves full time to the movement. In many cases their worldly skills, such as engineering or accountancy, prove very useful to the movement.

In summary, although the movement was founded by a man it is a woman's movement and capitalizes on feminine attributes. Women are held to have greater mystical powers than men, although their role is partly disguised by institutionalized possession. Prsonal inspiration is permissible within trance under the guise of a male spirit speaking. In such circumstances the woman herself is described as being a naive and simple soul. Moreover, women are still thought to be ritually pollutant during menstruation. They cannot during that time prepare *toli*, that is, consecrated food, or 'sit on Baba's chair', i.e. take meditation classes.

Thus, the restrictions of society are not altogether overcome within the movement. Apart from the principle of celibacy, the roles played by brothers and sisters are akin to those of husband and wife, one can at least understand the basis of outsiders' suspicions that the Brahma Kumaris centres are dens of sexual immorality, except that the original institution receives a twist in that the *men* seem to be playing the part of wives and the *women* that of husbands. It is ironic to find women using traditional male ploys in arguing their helplessness in household matters and stressing the spiritual nature of their interests.

I suggest that female power within the movement depends upon a hidden or unacknowledged male presence which enables the family structure to be inverted.

This in turn depends upon the principle of celibacy being observed. Furthermore this celibate, role-reversed family is linked to millennialist ideas which play an important part in their belief system (see n.3). Millennialism or the belief in the imminent destruction of the world remains the requirement for the procreation of the species. Bryan Wilson has written that 'Millennialism ... presents ... a vision of a different social order' (1973:7). I suggest that it also places a lighter burden on new patterns of social relationships in that they are not required to endure the test of time. However, the Brahma Kumaris are and have been able to draw upon those features of Hinduism which are to their advantage and to capitalize upon the export of Indian religions to the West, thereby sharing in some of the freedom of Western women. Rather than acting as a conservative force, religion has in this instance paved the way for social change, and the movement as a whole is viewed as a threat to traditional roles and institutions.

Notes

1.   The movement presents a different face in India and in the West. Whereas religious teaching in India incorporates many of the elements of traditional Hinduism (see note 3), this is down-played in the presentation of the movement in Western contexts. The millennialist beliefs which play a very prominent role in India are hardly mentioned in the West. Indeed, at any of the fairs and exhibitions organized by the Brahma Kumaris, posters depicting the end of the world are displayed everywhere. Also, in deference to the fact that Westerners find celibacy a difficult principle to accept, or, even understand, this too is given little mention. At conferences organized in the West the movement is presented to newcomers as being principally concerned with meditation and cultivating correct attitudes of mind. Although meditation is undoubtedly important in Brahma Kumari practice, the exclusion of other aspects of their belief system does give the movement an altogether different character.

2.   Hindu scriptures deny women any independent ritual status on account of their ritual impurity which stems from the polluting aspects of menstruation and childbirth and perhaps of ' female sexuality' as such. The consequences of these ideas has been that women have not been able to participate fully in religious life. Among the sects the situation has not improved. For example, the Hare Krishna movement accords women a very much restricted role (Judah 1974:86-7).

3.   The body of spiritual knowledge is very detailed and exact. It is a self-reinforcing and mutually interlocking system of ideas. The Brahma Kumaris publish a correspondence course on their belief system and numerous books and pamphlets both in Hindi and English which can be consulted.

The Brahma Kumaris begin their teaching by introducing newcomers to their perception of the soul and the supreme soul. Shiv Baba is seen as possessing all the attributes of perfection, love, purity and power, bliss and peace. He is not described as the creator of the universe or *kalpa* tree, which is eternal, but rather as its recreator. He enables souls through yoga or union with him to achieve perfection and thus acquire the 'passport for entry to the golden age'. The souls of mortals share in the attributes of the divine soul, but their original qualities have become tarnished and thus they must rediscover their original perfection through the fire of yoga. The concept of *karma* too plays an important part in Brahma Kumaris thought. Karma is a doctrine both of determinism and freedom. It is deterministic in the sense that one's present situation and personality or *samskaras* are seen as the fruit of past action. But equally one's future state depends upon the actions and store of *samskaras* which are laid down in the present. Hence, the importance of purifying and perfecting the soul by ridding oneself of vices. These five vices are referred to frequently and always in the same order: sex lust, anger, greed, attachment, and ego. The life of a yogi leaves these vices behind.

Perhaps the most complicated and detailed aspect of their belief system relates to the cosmic cycle which is represented as a *kalpa* tree. The point at which the cycle is conventionally entered is the golden age, which began precisely 5000 years ago. This was an age of pure happiness when men had no need of religion because they themselves were gods. This lasted 2500 years, and during this period men and women took eight births. Then came the silver age which lasted 1250 years when men took 12 births. An example of the precision involved in the beliefs is that the silver age is described as being 80% complete as opposed to the golden age which is 100% complete and pure. The copper age is the period during which the world religions are said to have started. During this period there are 21 births. The iron age reigns at present where man is seen as being totally corrupt and his soul rusted. During this period 42 births are taken. However, this latter part of the iron age is also described as an age of confluence which will usher in the golden age.

Thanks to the incarnation of Shiv Baba in Bapdada souls have been given the opportunity to purify themselves and to prepare themselves for their roles as deities in the golden age and to proceed straight to the golden age after a suitable period of purification. A further 9 *lakhs* will follow. This golden age will be ushered in by a nuclear holocaust and those who have led a pure life will then gain their rightful inheritance. In fact it is specified that 108 souls will have attained a sufficient degree of purity to be examples for others. Unlike the more orthodox Hindu belief, the Brahma Kumaris do not believe in the possibility of release from the cycle of rebirth. After the nuclear destruction of mankind there will be a temporary withdrawal to

Paramdam, but only to refresh and purify the soul before returning to the golden age. Thus the main points at which the Brahma Kumaris doctrine diverges from Hinduism are the following: firstly, Shiva seems to have a more paternal role with elements borrowed from Christianity. Secondly, their idea of a world cycle is very precise. Thirdly, they predict certain destruction with a few chosen ones saved. Fourthly, there is no escape from the cycle of rebirth.

The Brahma Kumaris do celebrate Hindu festivals, but they claim not to really believe in them and to celebrate them with a greater understanding. However, the festivals are marked by the giving of *toli* (consecrated food), *drishti* (blessing), picnics and dancing. Frequently I was given the apologetic excuse that the festival was being celebrated simply to demonstrate to me what happened amongst devout Hindus in the rest of India. Nevertheless, I gained the definite impression that it was an opportunity for celebration which was very much welcomed by all. Hindu festivals are also an opportunity for teaching the uninitiated the secrets of Brahma Kumari learning. For example, on the occasion of Krishna's birthday (21 August) an exhibition was staged in the museum in the centre of Mount Abu and attracted a steady flow of visitors throughout the day, perhaps partly because Mount Abu offers little else in the way of entertainment. The museum offered the usual display of pictorial representation of the world cycle and the *kalpa* tree, but in addition there were live representations of Krishna and Rada portrayed by small children against a background of the golden age. Dadi and Didi were put in a swing and dressed as deities. Two brothers sat above them dressed as Lakshmi and Narayan. At first there was singing and then dancing with men dancing with men and women with women.

The other Hindu festival which was celebrated during my visit and one which is probably considered to be the most important by the Brahma Kumaris is *Rakshi Bandan* which takes place on 15 August. Originally *rakhi* was tied by Indra's wife as a symbol of protection against devils. The Brahma Kumaris tie *rakhi* on all the brothers and sisters and use it as a symbol for combatting the vices as they understand them, particularly sex lust. The occasion stands out as being of prime importance in their religious calendar. The very direct and personal contact which exists between the elder sisters and all members of the community is also emphasized. On the occasion of *Rakshi Bandan* all write letters to Didi and Dadi describing the personal efforts which they have made towards self-realization and perfection. This involves enumerating what each feels to be his personal weaknesses, the techniques employed to overcome them and the success or otherwise attendant upon their endeavours. This aspect of their religious activity provides support for David Pocock's point that the importance given to an individual's relationship with a guru provides 'courage to the individual conscience' (1973:163).

The movement is also known as Raja Yoga. Raja Yoga means godly yoga. In Hindi the term yoga literally means union and in the religious context it means union with the divine soul or principle. There are different varieties of yoga; the most widely known is hatha yoga or body yoga. Hatha literally means penance, and union examining the experience of women sannyasins within two opposing historical contexts: a) the *bhakti yoga* tradition in Hinduism; b) the Women's Movement in the West.

Bhakti yoga as a 'feminine' path

In Hinduism there are many *yogas*, paths to *moksha* (liberation or enlightenment), but the predominant popular path is bhakti yoga. This is an ancient spiritual path in India, going back at least to the era of the Upanishads, peaking in the sixteenth century with Kabir and Nanak, and reviving again this century after a temporary eclipse under Islam and Christianity. Central to the practice is devotion to god – usually mediated and represented by the *guru* (teacher or master). The spiritual seeker finds a master and becomes initiated by him as his (usually his) disciple.

Historically discipleship in India has been confined almost exclusively to men, women being considered ignorant, impure, and generally inferior. Despite the existence of powerful goddesses and a number of holy women, some very famous (such as Meerabai), women's participation in religion has been mainly limited to domestic rituals. *Moksha* was not possible in a female body; at best a woman could hope for rebirth into a male body in order to pursue the spiritual path.

Yet paradoxically bhakti yoga can be viewed as a feminine path: devotional, heart-centred, valuing love and intuition above the intellect:

> [in some bhakti traditions] a woman was paradigmatic as devotee when the supreme deity was male. Thus, for a *male* devotee to enter into 'marriage mysticism' with a *male* god, he had to assume the psychology of a woman in love. (Young in Sharma 1987: 77)

This sometimes went as far as transvestism, especially in the cult of Chaitanya. In this century Ramakrishna took on the feminine role for six months so effectively that the village women accepted him as a woman (Leslie in Holden 1983: 103).

Feminism in the 1970s

Meanwhile, in the West during the 1970s, feminism was advocating transformation for women and society through political activism. In terms of gender roles, there was a strong reaction away from traditional female stereotypes towards emulating and even surpassing male achievements. Masculine values were normative, so this was the obvious path to equality and liberation. Nowadays it is easier for a woman to affirm 'feminine' values, though balancing 'masculine' and 'feminine' traits can still be a dilemma (Carol Christ and Judith Plaskow analyse it well in the Introduction to *Womanspirit Rising*, 1979). But at the time this option would have been regarded as regressive.

A number of women sannyasins were former feminists, and I was interested in what factors led to such an unpredictable transition. One of the main criticisms of the Women's Movement voiced by the ex-feminists I interviewed, and by other sannyasins (*Osho Times International* 1991), was its aggression and over-emphasis on the intellectual at the expense of the experiential. On the 'left' there was a strong opposition between politics and personal development. Feminism saw the personal as also political, so consciousness raising (CR) was on the agenda, but mainly as a means to a social end. As a result, women who were interested primarily in psychospiritual growth during this period tended to move into the Human Potential Movement (see above).

The 'defection' of several founder members of the British Women's Movement into the Rajneesh movement caused quite a stir, and in 1977 *Spare Rib* interviewed one of these women, who tried to explain her 'conversion':

> [Bhagwan] says it is the logical thinking, organised, rational, male mind which prevents one from experiencing oneself, and one's physical being and sensations and feelings. My mind, I realise, is conditioned totally, 99%, by what you could call a sort of patriarchal mind, a desire to be logical, realistic, materialist. ... Now I see trying to work out women's problems through the 'male' mind to be destructive and useless (Fell 1977).

This passage was denounced by the feminist writer Jill Tweedie as illustrating:

> the barmy acceptance by some women and even some militant feminists that the qualities men have described as 'female' through the centuries are essentially correct and only need dusting off and polishing up to take their rightful place in a deprived society. Men lay claim to rational thought and their claims are believed by women. So all that women have to do is claim equal rights for feminine emotion (or, in the case of Bhagwan followers, exalt emotion's superiority) and all in the women's world will be well ... What all this amounts to is a brainwashing campaign by men of women and women of themselves upon a truly staggering scale (1977:149).

This exchange sets the scene, and draws up the battle lines!

Thirteen years later I interviewed the subject of the *Spare Rib* article, who elaborated on why she had 'taken sannyas':

What took me into feminism was a search ... Feminism helped me to understand how I'd been conditioned as a woman, but the main thing about conditioning is collusion. I saw conditioning, but I didn't say, 'Wicked people conditioning me, it's their fault.' What I saw is that as women we allow ourselves to be conditioned, and what has to be changed is the mechanism through which we allow ourselves to be conditioned. ... When I met someone who saw conditioning on a much wider scale than just conditioning of women, there was no intellectual change for me. It was following the same path, because it's my allowing myself to be conditioned which is the problem.

Surrendering to a male master

'Taking sannyas' involved a requirement of 'surrendering' to Osho as one's spiritual master. This is traditional in bhakti yoga, but provoked much criticism in the West, challenging deeply held concepts of the ultimate value of self-determination, individuality, democracy. In the Women's Movement religion in general was viewed as irredeemably patriarchal, and surrender to a male master was the ultimate indignity.

Here is the reply of one former feminist spokeswoman to the question how the idea of taking on a male master struck her.

It didn't strike me with much difficulty, but it did to a lot of my friends – a man's picture around my neck! But I'd been moving away for some time from feminism. I found that it was restricting me and my development spiritually. And also when I looked at the truth of my life, I found that the people who really mattered to me were my son and my lover. Feminism didn't give me a framework to explain this. Also for a long time I'd been getting more involved in humanistic psychology, so I was really looking at stuff that wasn't really being given a place in feminism.

The idea might have been difficult, but it was too strong energetically. His voice came and hit me, and this man, as I saw it, offered me a pathway to liberation. I can't explain easily, but I felt my heart open, and the exhaustion of all these years trying to understand. Here was someone who spoke to me directly.

Beyond gender

Another reason both men and women gave for being untroubled by the idea of surrendering to a man was that many of them saw Osho as in some sense androgynous, or 'beyond gender', as in the following three examples:

> I didn't really see him as a person, I just saw him as a being, radiating love.

> I never saw him as a man to whom I would as a woman surrender – that wasn't the relationship. It was very clear that he was beyond being a man or a woman – he was all love and receptivity.

> On the one hand he could be roaring at you: you'd really feel the wrath of god pouring down ... And then in the next moment he could be so gentle that you felt you were being caressed by the lightest, softest thing in the world. ... At times I saw him as a cosmic dancer, not having any sex but drawing you closer and closer to him through this incredible mixture of male and female qualities.

This view was widespread among disciples, almost an article of faith, though I found some scepticism among ex-disciples. One in particular who had been deeply involved in politics and feminism found traces of unreconstructed male ego in Osho:

> Whenever he would talk about meditation and spiritual stuff, that was fine with me, but if he talked about outside stuff – politics or women – I couldn't go along with it ... All his experiences were male experiences, and everything was always 'he'. It didn't really disturb me because I thought, well, he's a man, and he's been brought up in a male-dominated society. It didn't really take away from the content of what he was talking about for me, though it jarred a little bit.

Celebrating the feminine

A large part of Osho's appeal to women and men disciples was his celebration of femininity:

> Rejoice in your feminine qualities, make a poetry of your feminine qualities ... I would like the whole world to be full of feminine qualities.

In Osho's view, in line with bhakti yoga, the greatest spiritual virtues – such as love, trust, devotion, intuition – were feminine in nature. Not only did he promote this view in the abstract, but he claimed that women embodied and expressed these qualities more naturally and easily than men. Therefore, they made the best disciples. In a sense, this can be seen as a logical move from the bhakti yoga view of men as 'carrying' the feminine at least in the spiritual realm: a natural marriage of Western ideas of gender with Eastern spirituality. But in the Indian context it was a radical step.

My interviewees tended to endorse this viewpoint, though some were a bit hesitant, and some emphasized that men were equally capable of this kind of discipleship. Here are two examples:

> I like the way he boosted the women ... I could understand what he said in a way ... the way he operated drew forth the devotee quality, didn't it, so I guess he liked women for that because they could be with him more easily. At the same time I think he drew that feminine quality out of men.

> I feel that because of their femininity being more to the fore, [women] are probably much more open initially, much less ego probably to say yes to a master than a man. ... We're much more in touch with our feelings, our heart and intuition.

Whether or not they felt women made better disciples, almost every woman I spoke to felt that in some way her sense of herself *as a woman* had been endorsed:

> One thing that happened as a sannyasin was that the side of myself that was combative, felt I had to assert myself as a woman against men, making me rather aggressive and masculine, I was more and more able to shed. I could see what was truly beautiful about being a woman – not to be subservient, but powerful in receptivity.

Another woman said:

> I didn't have any sense of myself as a woman before sannyas. I felt like a shrivelled bud, not even a flower – the bud hadn't even been able to start flowering. And through sannyas it feels like this bud is slowly opening, the life force is coming into it.

In contrast, another woman, who had suffered as a child from pressure to excel academically by her scientist father, described the process in terms more secular – even profane, in the Durkheimian sense:

> I could relax, and didn't have to prove I was as good as a man. It was OK to just do female things like cleaning, cooking, housework. I enjoyed it and could admit I enjoyed it. I didn't have to be a scientist, lawyer, doctor or something.

Women in power in the Rajneesh ashram

The above section constitutes a brief outline of the experiential, psychospiritual dimension of female discipleship, which gives expression to the more traditionally 'feminine' aspect. An examination of the social organization of the ashram reveals a very different picture: a kind of spiritual matriarchy.

It should be borne in mind that in almost all religions, old and new, women have very little spiritual or temporal power. The few sociological studies undertaken of gender roles in new religious movements (NRMs) reveal a depressing consensus on the low status of women throughout these movements: Christian, Eastern, and even New Age, often endorsed by an implicitly or explicitly misogynist theology (Harder 1974; Jacobs 1984; Aidala 1985; Rose 1987).

The Rajneesh movement has not been included in any comparative studies of women in NRMs. Most of the literature on this movement pays scant attention to gender roles, apart from noting the preponderance of women in leadership roles. There are only three studies, all unpublished, which consider the issues in detail: Carl Latkin's PhD thesis on Rajneeshpuram (1987); Marion Goldman's study on women high achievers at Rajneeshpuram (1988); and Susan Palmer's comparative study of women in the Rajneesh movement, ISKCON, and the Unification Church (1987).

From Osho's teaching two opposite ideals of femininity can be extrapolated: on the one hand woman as devotee, surrendered, merged into the master, the commune, the work; on the other hand woman freed of the shackles of centuries-old conditioning, reclaiming her power. His own much quoted statement of the latter ideal is:

> My own vision is that the coming age will be the age of the woman. Man has tried for 5000 years and has failed. Now a chance has to be given to the woman. Now she should be given the reins of all the powers. She should be given an opportunity to bring her feminine energies to function, to work.

The question, then, is how far this affirmation, even celebration, of women and feminine values, can be taken at face value, and how far it was an exploitation of the traditional receptivity, passivity, and submissiveness of women. There are different views on this, and motivation is hard to pin down. [But externally, the Rajneesh ashram conformed to the 'charismatic' model of authority, in that all the spiritual and most of the temporal power was concentrated in the master alone at the top of the hierarchy. However, as the movement grew, to the point where there were over 2000 people working and many more doing the programmes, Osho deputized more and more of his secular powers – mostly to women. Almost every department was headed with God is achieved through discipline of the body. Other forms of yoga provide mantras as an aid to concentration and to deflect attention from bodily concerns. Raja yoga does not empty the mind of thoughts nor does it deny bodily concerns but it concentrates on the idea of the eternal soul and the qualities of one's own soul which share in the character of eternity. In general yoga is a technique for shortening the cycle of rebirth.

4.   Within Hinduism ideas about purity and pollution play a very important part; indeed, they underpin the caste system. An aspect of this concern with purity is the importance attached to celibacy. Hinduism has a strongly developed concept of the life cycle. This concept is of four distinct stages of life which comprise the *varnashrama*. The first stage is that of the scholar living in a monastic order – the *brahmacharya*; the second is that of the husband, father and householder or *grihastha*; the third stage involves withdrawal from the physical and social world and is called *vanaprastha*; and the fourth stage is that of the *sannyasi* who has totally renounced this world and travels around with a begging bowl. The two points I want to make are firstly that it is a male life cycle and there is no counterpart elaborating the stages of women's spiritual development. Women's spiritual lives are static by comparison. Secondly, celibacy is a prerequisite of all but one of the stages, namely, that of *grihastha* . Thus within Hinduism celibacy is highly valued. The Brahma Kumaris pointed out that an old man only has to declare himself celibate to be called a *sannyasi* and to be highly revered. Within Hinduism there is a concept of the *kalinga* which is depicted as a snake of semen which coils its way along the spine transporting energy from the genital region to the brain. The *kalinga* provides a simple representation of a very widespread idea and, of course, denies the importance of celibacy for women.

References

A.S. Altekar (1938; reprinted 1973) *The Position of Women in Hindu Civilization,* Delhi: Motilal Banarsidass

Edwin Ardener (1975) Belief and the Problem of Women, in *Perceiving Women,* Shirley Ardener (ed.), London: Malaby Press

Lawrence Babb (1975) *The Divine Hierarchy: A Perspective for Understanding Society,* New York & Toronto: The Edwin Mellen Press

S. C. Dube (1963) Men's and Women's Roles in India: a Sociological Review, in *Women in New Asia,* B.E. Ward (ed.) 174-203, Paris: Unesco.

Ann Charlotte Eschermann (1973) Religion, Reaction and Change: The Role of Sects in Hinduism, unpublished paper presented at the International Workshop Seminar on Religion and Development in Asian Societies, in Kandy, Sri Lanka

Clifford Geertz (1975) *Islam Observed: Religious Development in Morocco and Indonesia,* New Haven & London: Yale University Press

William James (1902) *The Varieties of Religious Experience: A Study in Human Nature,* (1960 edition) London: Fontana

J. Stillson Judah (1974) *Hare Krishna and the Counter Culture,* New York: Wiley

David Kopf (1979) *The Brahmo Samaj and the Shaping of the Modern India Mind,* New Jersey: Princeton University Press

Henry C. Lea (1884) *Sacerdotal Celibacy in the Christian Church,* Boston: Houghton Miffen & Co

Julia Leslie (1983) Essence and Existence: Women and Religion in Ancient Indian Texts, in *Women's Religious Experience,* Pat Holden (ed.), London: Croom Helm

Thomas C. Oden (1982) The Intensive Group Experience: the New Pietism, in *New Religious Movements,* Eileen Barker (ed.) New York & Toronto: The Edwin Mellen Press

David Pocock (1973) *Mind, Body and Wealth,* Oxford: Basil Blackwell

Ashok Rudra (1975) Cultural and Religious Influences, in *Indian Women,* Jain Devaki (ed.) pp.39-49. Government of India, Delhi, Publications Division

Roy Wallis (1978) *The Rebirth of the Gods? Reflections on the New Religions in the West,* inaugural lecture, Queen's University of Belfast

Bryan Wilson (1973) *Magic and the Millennium,* London: Heinemann

5

Devotees and Matriarchs: women sannyasins in the Rajneesh movement

ELIZABETH PUTTICK

'Sannyas' and the Human Potential Movement

From the mid-1970s to the early 1980s, the Rajneesh movement was the most fashionable of the many new religious movements (NRMs) on offer. Its leader, formerly known as Bhagwan Shree Rajneesh and latterly as Osho, was born in India in 1931, and became 'enlightened' at the age of 21. After leaving his post as Professor of Philosophy at the University of Jabalpur in 1966 he travelled throughout India, attracting huge audiences and followers with his controversial discourses on religion, sex and politics. After a while the most devoted core of the following became formalized into 'sannyas', an adaptation of the traditional Indian master-disciple relationship. In the early 1970s Westerners began joining, and by 1974, when Osho set up an ashram in Poona, the Western sannyasins outnumbered the Indians.

Like most NRMs, the appeal of this movement was primarily to women and men in the educated middle classes, in their late twenties to thirties. Often they had 'dropped out' of society, but out of disillusion rather than failure (cf. Volinn 1985). Part of this disillusion was with the lack of spiritual nourishment they found in the Judaeo-Christian tradition, which they described as dry, boring, dead, lacking in meaning and inspiration. Yet materialism and scientific rationalism did not provide answers or fulfilment. On the other hand, drugs had often provided glimpses of alternative realities and even ecstasy, and became triggers to a search for spiritual experience not dependent on chemical stimulus.

Counter-cultural 'seekers' who had reached this stage often experimented with meditation, sometimes joining an NRM in the process. One of the main differences between the Rajneesh movement and other NRMs was the influence upon it of the Human Potential Movement (HPM), from which many members were drawn. The HPM is an umbrella term comprising a range of psychotherapies such as encounter groups, primal therapy, bioenergetics and rebirthing, some of which have themselves been classified as NRMs (Heelas 1982). Much has been written about the HPM (eg. Rowan 1976), mainly in terms of its emphasis on 'self-realization' and 'peak experiences', but one of its most significant aspects here is its reawakening of the repressed 'feminine'. After two world wars Western society had become militarized to the point where it was difficult for people to express any spontaneous feeling. Discipline was the primary virtue, and austerity the climate. So the post-war generation grew up economically privileged but emotionally deprived. The HPM affirmed such values as relationship, feeling, tenderness, connection, and intuition – traditional female qualities, which are only now beginning to be given any positive value within the wider society.

Among the first Western sannyasins were the leaders of the HPM in Britain, Paul and Patricia Lowe, who founded the 'growth centre' Quaesitor and became sannyasins in 1972. Patricia, renamed Ma Anand Poonam, ran the main British centres until 1984 (see below). Following them, many of the best known group leaders in Europe and America joined the movement, closely followed by their own group participants. The HPM was thus the source of the main influx into the movement, though people also joined for other reasons. Whatever their motivations, sannyasins were almost invariably drawn to Eastern mysticism and meditation techniques. Even if they had not consciously been seeking a master, becoming a disciple to Osho was experienced as the culmination of their search.

About 60 per cent of sannyasins were women, and it is their experience in particular that I have been researching. The master-disciple relationship, especially in its aspect of the surrender of women devotees to a male master, was the most contentious and even offensive aspect of NRMs to feminists. I therefore begin by

One thing it did was give me the experience of being invulnerable, so I lost touch with my vulnerability. But it was a very heady experience, like a drug ... and when I came off it I really crashed, because I did really think I was special. I did have an inner hierarchy, and I was very keen on moving towards the top of it. I got caught up in the power system.

Asked if she thought women had any particular qualities for these positions, she replied:

Well, they poisoned people instead of shooting them, and they sneakily wiretapped instead of having bar-room brawls ... I think power does the same things to women as to men, it's just a different form. Maybe women had to have that experience of power after so long of being powerless, relatively ... Maybe in some collective sense it had to be balanced, and for an individual woman to become whole she would have to go through the experience of power, because it's a part of being alive and it's a hard one for a woman to get.

Other people felt allowance should be made for women's inexperience, after millennia of repression:

I think when you've been submissive and you first start being assertive, it comes over very raw, bossy. I've mellowed out a lot now, but I think at the time it was my suppressed stuff coming out.

Finding a feminine style of leadership

However, despite these traumatic events, sannyasin women do claim to have learned valuable lessons through the exercise of power, and through experiencing both sides of the fence. A previous cleaner reported:

I had difficulty with the powerful women in the ashram ... When I came back [my lover] and I ran Kalptaru for a while, so I did have to get into my powerful self. That was lovely, very good to get into that.

Asked if she had felt any conflict with the receptive, devotional side she had described earlier, she replied:

No, why not? It just felt different aspects, somehow. It felt all part of just becoming more me, bigger, moving out of the little, constricted me into a bigger one.

74

Another example was a woman who initially had very hostile feelings about the women in power in Medina, but then discovered a different style of leadership for herself:

> I hated them, loathed them ... because they were bitchy, arrogant, nasty, full of themselves, ugly, unfeminine ... I wanted to be myself, find my own strength, but definitely not be like that.

When she ended up running the London centre, she felt she had found a way of being a leader without losing her femininity:

> I was into having fun, enjoying myself ... I wasn't into being a boss, I was into expressing my creativity. The boss bit was completely irrelevant, the point was to be there and express myself as fully as I possibly could with my friends. I think it worked. I never had a heavy moment, or very occasionally. I was supposed to be a 'Mum', but mostly I felt we were all in it together.

Several women referred to 'motherliness' as an important feminine quality. Whereas men's names were prefixed with Swami ('master of oneself'), women's were prefixed with Ma ('mother'). The nurturing aspect of motherhood was seen as very important in the work, especially for the coordinators. At Rajneeshpuram this became semi-formalized, and all female coordinators were known as 'moms'. (And informally, the female leadership was dubbed the 'ma-archy'). Even Sheela was known as the 'mother' of the 'family' of Rajneeshpuram (Fitzgerald 1986, 279), though with hindsight she may be perceived as more like the 'bad mother' of Freudian psychology. This tendency was also noted by Palmer (1987) at Rajneeshpuram, as well as its corollary: 'Commune members often refer to themselves as "kids", presided over by the "moms" and "supermoms". "I'll have to ask my mom", replied one thirty-year-old swami when I asked if he could take off a morning free "worship" to be interviewed'.

The Rajneesh movement today
The Rajneesh movement is now based in Poona again and claims to be expanding, despite the death of Osho in 1990. However, there seems to be a general feeling of disillusion with the feminine after the experiences of Rajneeshpuram. It was widely felt that the surrendered devotee ideal encouraged and supported an extreme passivity

and submission that allowed the abuses and exploitation of Rajneeshpuram. Some people also felt that giving women the opportunity to have power and responsibility had not worked: women turned out to be no better at it than men, in some ways worse, especially without the checks and balances that 'left-brained' rationality and democratic structures might have provided. However, I did not come across anyone who blamed female incapacity for power in general, as against individual women, for the failure.

At the same time, some women were genuinely trying to develop a more intuitive, nurturing, 'right-brained' style of leadership – which has now become an approved management style. They were experimenting with exercising authority without sacrificing their femininity and becoming imitation men. This is a dilemma that faces all women today in positions of power, whether spiritual or secular, and there is clearly no easy answer.

It seems that the move now is towards a more natural equality and balance between male and female in the work situation – away from positive discrimination and towards democracy.

Another point to be remembered is that the heyday of the Rajneesh movement was before the days of the women's spirituality movement and ecofeminism, so positive spiritual options for women were limited. The predominant view among current and ex-sannyasins is that despite the collective failure of Rajneeshpuram, important lessons were learned and benefits gained. It was widely seen as one of the first attempts to 'revision' the feminine, which gave women the opportunity on the one hand to reclaim their femininity, and on the other hand to experience power and leadership to a degree rare even in the secular world, and far beyond the scope of most other new religious movements.

References

Angela Aidala (1985) Social change, gender roles, and new religious movements, *Sociological Analysis 46 (3)*, 287-314

Kirk Braun (1984) *Rajneeshpuram: the Unwelcome Society,* West Linn, OR: Scout Creek Press

Lewis Carter (1990) *Charisma and Control in Rajneeshpuram,* Cambridge: Cambridge University Press

Carol Christ and Judith Plaskow (eds), (1979) *Womanspirit Rising,* San Francisco: Harper & Row

Alison Fell (1977) All a Girl Needs is a Guru, *Spare Rib*, 59, 6-10

Frances Fitzgerald (1986) *Cities on a Hill: A Journey through American Subcultures,* NY: Simon & Schuster

Marion Goldman (1988) The Women of Rajneeshpuram, *CSWS Review,* University of Oregon, 18-21

Mary W Harder (1974) Sex Roles in the Jesus Movement, *Social Compass,* 21 (3), 345-53

Paul Heelas (1982) Californian self-religions and socializing the subjective, in Eileen Barker (ed.), *New Religious Movements: a perspective for understanding society,* New York: Edwin Mellen Press, 69-85

Janet Jacobs (1984) The economy of love in religious commitment: the deconversion of women from nontraditional religious movements, *Journal for the Scientific Study of Religion,* 23(2), 155-71

Vasant Joshi (1982) *The Awakened One: the Life and Work of Bhagwan Shree Rajneesh,* San Francisco: Harper & Row

Carl A Latkin (1987) Rajneeshpuram, Oregon: an exploration of gender and work roles, self-concept and psychological well-being in an experimental community, unpublished PhD thesis, Univ.Oregon

Julia Leslie (1983) Essence and existence: women and religion in ancient Indian texts, in *Women's Religious Experience* (ed. Pat Holden), London: Croom Helm

Osho Times International (1991), 4 (16)

Susan Palmer (1987) Women in New Spiritual Communes: Rajneesh Lovers, Moon Sisters, Krishna Mothers, paper presented to the Society for the Scientific Study of Religion, Louisville

Susan Rose (1987) Women warriors: the negotiation of gender in a charismatic community, *Sociological Analysis* 48(3), 245-58

John Rowan (1976) *Ordinary Ecstasy: Humanistic Psychology in Action,* London: RKP

Jill Tweedie (1980) *In the Name of Love,* London: Granada

Katherine Young (1987) Hinduism, in *Women in World Religions* (ed Arvind Sharma New York: State Univ. of New York

Ernest Volinn (1985) Eastern meditation groups: why join? *Sociological Analysis,* 46:2, 147-56

6

Daughter of Fire by IRINA TWEEDIE

Documentation & experiences of a modern Naqshbandi Sufi

SARA SVIRI

Introduction

The Sufi Path (*tariqa*) known as the *naqshbandiyya* derives its name from the fourteenth-century mystic Muhammad ibn Muhammad Baha' al-Din an-Naqshbandi (d. 1389) (Trimingham 1971: 62ff, 93ff, and passim; Schimmel 1975: 363ff; ter Haar 1992: 311-21). However, the chroniclers of this Sufi path, and subsequently also the hagiographers of the Sufi *tariqas* at large, link the *naqshbandiyya* with a lineage, or chain (*silsila*), which goes back to the twelfth-century master Yusuf al-Hamadhani (d.1140). The latter – to quote from a modern English redaction of some traditional sources – 'occupies a position of extraordinary importance in Turkish Sufism [i.e., the Sufi Paths which originated in Turkestan in Central Asia, since he represents the "top link" from which the "chains" of several major Orders are suspended'[1] (Shushud 1983; Bennett 1977: 121ff). These two Sufi teachers, known also as *khwajagan* ('masters') (Trimingham 1971: 14; ter Haar 1992: 312), together with a third master – 'Abd al-Khaliq al-Ghujdawani (d. 1220) – are traditionally regarded as those who had the deepest impact on the evolution of the *naqshbandiyya* in its distinctive ways.

All three of them, in their own ways played an important role in introducing the eleven principles by which the *naqshbandiyya* came to be distinguished from the other Sufi Paths.[2] The first and foremost of these was the silent recollection of God, i.e. the silent meditation (*dhikr khafi*).[3] In most Sufi Paths and fraternities the ancient practice of rhythmic vocal repetitions of the Divine Names, and in particular of the most sacred name *allah*, evolved into a ceremonial audition (*sama*),[4] sometimes referred to as a 'spiritual recital', aimed at inducing ecstasy and higher states of consciousness.[5] Although most Sufi teachers urged their disciples to prefer the inner remembrance of the heart (*dhikr qalbi*) over and above the audible remembrance of the tongue (*dhikr bi-l-lisan*), no other path besides the *naqsbandiyya* practised exclusively the silent *dhikr*. This is why its followers have been known as 'the silent Sufis'.[6]

It would appear that the elevated rank accorded by the *naqshbandi* masters to the silent meditation, and their abstention from auditions, loud invocations and chanting, were not simply due to their rigid pietism or ascetic tendencies, but to an esoteric understanding of the capacity, through the silent *dhikr*, of the merging of the heart with the Divine Silence.[7]

The *naqshbandi* line of Sufism, originally based in the Muslim provinces of Central Asia, was introduced into India in the sixteenth century via a disciple of 'Ubaidallah Ahrar (d.1490), one of the great *naqshbandi* masters of Central Asia. His centre was in Tashkent (then known as Shash), but he had exerted tremendous influence in spreading the *naqshbandi* teaching in two new geographical directions: westwards to Anatolia (the Turkish branch) and south-eastwards to India. The most influential master of the Indian *naqshbandi* lineage, a mystic of great acclaim among Sufis and Orthodox Muslims alike, was Sheikh Ahmad Sirhindi from east Punjab (d. 1624). His spiritual and religious impact on Muslim India at the threshold of the second Islamic Millennium was acknowledged by the honorary title bestowed on him: *mujaddid-i alf-i thani* (the Renewer of the Second Millennium).[8] Those who followed in Sheikh Sirhindi's footsteps became known as the *Naqshbandiyya-Mujaddidiyya*.

It is to this Indian branch of the *naqshbandi* lineage that Irina Tweedie, through her teacher Bhai Sahib and through his teacher Guru Maharaj, is connected.

This brief introduction is intended not only as a historical framework for Irina Tweedie's affiliation with the Indian *naqshbandiyya*; it also wishes to emphasize the phenomenological principle, which lies at the root of all Sufi Paths, namely: that mystical schools exist and propagate by constituting an unbroken chain of transmission; an uninterrupted lineage, in which the esoteric teaching, as well as the exoteric practices and etiquettes, and the authority to guide the fraternity, are transmitted from master to disciple in consecutive links of successors.[9]   (This is not to say that all teachers and all teachings, even within the same Path, are uniform. It is understood that each successor works within their individual creative characteristics, as well as within their individual limitations, and in accordance with their own time and place). A significant feature of the *naqshbandiyya* in this respect is the fact that a direct link can sometimes be established between an adept of the Path and the spiritual power of a deceased master, either from the near or from the remote past. Thus the sources tell us that 'from the point of view of spiritual initiation Baha' al-Din Naqshband (d. 1389) is the true disciple and successor of 'Abd al-Khaliq Ghujduwani [d.1220; see above] although they never met' (ter Haar 1992: 315-16).

In one of their very first meetings, dated in Irina Tweedie's diary as 3rd October [1961], Bhai Sahib – the title by which her *naqshbandi* teacher from Kanpur was addressed – explains to her what Sufism is:

> Sufism is a way of life. It is neither a religion nor a philosophy. There are Hindu Sufis, Muslim Sufis, Christian Sufis – My Revered Guru Maharaj was a Muslim (*Daughter of Fire*, p.9).

This statement is significant. Bhai Sahib was a Hindu but received his *adhikara* (the authority to carry on the teaching; in Arabic: *ijaza*) from a Muslim teacher, and transmitted the *adhikara* to Irina Tweedie, an Orthodox Christian by birth. This statement implies an extension of the boundaries of Sufism. According to Bhai Sahib, this has been happening not only in the modern age, but since pre-Islamic times. In the entry of 25th December [1962] Tweedie records his words to her:

> Sufis were before the Prophet [Muhammad]. Sufism always was; it is the ancient Wisdom. Only before the Prophet they were not called Sufis. Only a few centuries after his death they were called Sufis (*ibid*, p.382).

Thus, the mystical teaching, or rather training, which Irina Tweedie records in her diary, draws from two polar yet complementary sources: the historical, time-bound framework of the tradition – exemplified by the lineage of the Path; and the truly mystic, esoteric aspect of the Path, which is understood to be timeless and beyond the boundaries of historical religions. This polarity can also be explored on a phenomenological-comparative level – a task that is beyond the scope of this paper.

The heart as the locum of the mystical journey in Sufism

What is a mystical Path? Sufis say: 'Our journey is the journey of the heart to God, the Beloved'. The 'mystical journey' is seen as an internal, psychological journey, which takes place within the human heart. Its goal or 'object' is 'the Divine Beloved', and the varied experiences of 'Love' become the stages and stations on the journey. Ibn 'Arabi, an Andalusian Sufi (d. 1240 in Damascus), usually better known for his esoteric *theosophical* mysticism than for his romantic poetry, writes in poetical eloquence:

> The goblet of love is the lover's heart, not his reason or his sense perception. For the heart fluctuates from state to state, just as God – who is the Beloved – is each day upon some task' (*Quran* 55:29). So the lover undergoes constant variation of the Beloved in His acts ... Love has many diverse and mutually opposed properties. Hence nothing receives these properties except that which has the capacity to fluctuate along with love. This belongs only to the heart (cited in Chittick 1989:108).

According to Sufi psychology the heart is an enigmatic and mysterious organ: on the one hand, Sufis say, the heart is nothing but 'a hollow piece of flesh – *bid' a jaufaa* [Arabic] – within the cavity of the body'; on the other hand, says a Sufi tradition, it is 'the treasurehouse of divine mysteries'. It is in the 'heart of hearts', in the innermost chamber of this spherical organ, whose centre is an ineffable point, that the human and the divine commune and unite. To this enclosed shrine no creature is allowed access. It is guarded zealously by the Divine Beloved Himself as a unique and priceless pearl, for the sole purpose of the communion with the human lover.

> A Sufi writer of the ninth century from Tirmidh in Khurasan (north-east Persia) writes: 'God placed the heart within the cavity of the human chest, and it belongs to God alone. No one has any claim on it. God holds the heart between two of his fingers, and no one may have access to it, neither an angel nor a prophet; no created being in the whole of creation. God alone turns it as He wishes. Within the heart God placed the knowledge of Him and He lit it with the Divine Light ... By this light He gave the heart eyes to see (Arberry 1947:116ff; Schimmel 1975:197).

The mystical journey therefore, and the mystical union, do not take place 'in the heavenly spheres' but in the deepest recesses of the human heart. 'The seven heavens and the seven earths', says a Sufi tradition, 'do not contain me; but the heart of my servant contains me (Schimmel 1975:190).

The mystical journey in the Sufi tradition is understood as a preparation for the communion between the human lover and the Divine Beloved. In the process of this preparation the 'hollow piece of flesh', sometimes referred to also as 'the dead piece of flesh', is revived. It is transformed into 'a clear and pure glass goblet'[10] made to contain a special kind of energy, an energy which is described variably as wine, water, blood, light, or fire; whose intensity is described in images of consuming and purifying fire, or of an effulgent light, and which is called love.

The transformation of the heart through the teacher

The task of this alchemical transformation is beyond the power of any human being. Sufis reiterate that human beings by their own efforts alone cannot accomplish the task of igniting the fire – the love-energy – which resides in their depths. At the same time it is also very rare that a man or a woman can transfer the intensity and passion of the love energy directly onto God. This is why a teacher is required.

Perhaps the best known instance in the history of Sufism of a teacher-disciple relationship, in which an immediate psychological transformation in the disciple occurred through the explosive energy transmitted by the teacher, is the case of Jalal al-Din Rumi and Shams-i Tabriz-i. When Rumi (d. 1273 in Konya, Anatolia) met Shams – an itinerary *darwish* who appeared one day in Konya, Rumi's hometown – he had been already a renowned Sufi teacher in his own right, a popular and sober mystic. In his Sufi training, which was conducted under the guidance of several teachers, including his own father, he went through the traditional preparatory stages. He exerted himself with rigorous practices, vigils, fasts, meditations, retreats. He made his 'vessels' ready: the clay container, the water, the oil, the wick (to use the image of a medieval oriental lamp). Everything was ready for the spark to kindle the wick, so that it could burn and produce heat and light.

The moment Jalal al-Din set eyes on Shams the devotional fire in his heart, which up until then had produced only a dim light, was all at once ignited. The result was a gushing poetic and didactic creativity, which never ceased flowing until his last days. The love energy which had become freed owing to the encounter with the 'reflection of the Beloved in a human form' has produced one of the subtlest and richest forms of mystical poetry – passionate, intense, and sensual, yet full of painful longing and intuitive wisdom.[11]

Shams did not 'teach' Rumi in any conventional sense; he was simply the catalyst through whom the love energy, dormant in the heart of hearts, became alive and dynamic. This could happen because Rumi saw in him the reflection of the Divine beauty and perfection. Only through this experience, which was as devastating as it was exalted, did Rumi himself become, for his own disciples, a true reflection of divine perfection, and thus a continuous source of mystical inspiration and a medium for their own transformation.

Thus the teacher in the Sufi tradition has a twofold function: to become the mirror in which the disciple sees the Divine reflection; and to use his energy in order to create the love energy in the heart of the disciple.

The teacher-disciple relationship and the transformation of the human heart through the love energy which is created in it are central themes in Sufi literature, both prose and poetry, from the eighth century onwards. These are also the pivotal themes of the modern account of the Sufi training which is the subject of this paper. This account is a first-hand description of the experiences of Irina Tweedie, Russian by birth, with her Hindu-Sufi teacher, to whom she refers as Bhai Sahib or Guruji. Her account was published twice: in an abridged form under the title *The Chasm of Fire* (1978); and in a complete and unabridged edition entitled *Daughter of Fire* (1986).

Daughter of Fire

When Irina Tweedie arrived at Kanpur in October 1961 to meet her future teacher, a Sufi of the *naqshbandiyya-mujaddidiyya* order (see above), she came as a proud, self-opinionated, somewhat condescending European lady, with a strong intellect and a temperamental character. However, an inner restlessness, stirred up by the loss of a husband whom she dearly loved, drove her all the way to India. This restlessness was coupled with a dim notion, derived from a vision far beyond the understanding of her own mind, of a link with an ancient tradition. When she returned to London in 1966, after the death of her teacher and a solitary retreat of several months in the Himalayas, she was – to use her own expression – 'as a person run over by a steam-roller'. What happens to a person who is run over by a steam-roller? S/he is flattened out, s/he is deflated, s/he loses her own features.

'To become featureless' is a well testified Sufi expression and experience, alluded to in many images and several terms. One of these terms is *fanaa* – 'annihilation'. It means the annihilation of 'the small within the great, the drop within the sea, the atom within the sun'.[12]   Another way of describing it is as merging, becoming absorbed. This was the culmination of the experiences which her teacher Bhai Sahib had 'given' her. 'I give you experiences', he told her, 'and you do with them what you want'.

At their very first meeting the teacher told her: 'I would like you to keep a diary, day-by-day entries of your experiences. And also to keep a record of your dreams .... Dreams are important; they are a guidance' (Tweedie 1986:12).   The diary, he told her, was necessary not as an outlet for her emotions, but as a document for other seekers: '"Keep a diary", said my teacher', Irina Tweedie writes in the Foreword to her book. '"One day it will become a book. But you must write it in such a way that it should help others. People say, such things did happen thousands of years ago – we read in books about it. This book will be a proof that such things do happen today as they happened yesterday and will happen tomorrow – to the right people, in the right time, and in the right place"' (Tweedie 1986:ix).

Access to the Sufi tradition is difficult because of the language barrier. Not many Westerners are familiar with Arabic, Persian, Urdu or Turkish. Moreover, the knowledge of these languages is not in itself sufficient for understanding this vast literature: the esoteric tradition is often couched in a smoke-screen of metaphorical allusions and poetic language which is temperamentally alien and ambiguous to most Western readers. Tweedie's book, in accordance with her teacher's instructions, was to be an up-to-date document, written in a direct, straightforward and modern language, accessible to many. Yet in this contemporary manner the ancient training and the stages of the journey towards the transformation of the heart were to be conveyed.

In the entry for 22nd August 1962 Tweedie records Bhai Sahib's words to her:

> Now is the time that you should note down all the experiences ... Doubts should be noted down too ... otherwise how will the solution be understood? It will serve for the book you will write. The experience you have, and will have in the future, you can find only in the Persian language, mostly in the form of poetry, and very little of it has been translated until now ... But you will write from your own proper experiences, living experiences (Tweedie 1986:265-6).

What does this document describe? What is the ancient tradition of a spiritual training which Tweedie, in a modern garb, records in her diary?

Sufism is a 'psychological' tradition. Its main concern as a mystical system is not metaphysical knowledge, nor eschatological fantasies of salvation or doom, but rather the subtle mapping of psychological fluctuations and the gradual unfolding of inner states of being. Sufi literature from as early as the ninth century has portrayed the struggle between the psychological components clustered around the 'ego' (*nafs*): the centre of the I-consciousness, and between the components of the non-ego, the Self, whose seat is the inner 'centre', the heart of hearts.

It is the pain and suffering ensuing from this constant struggle that constitute true effort on the part of the wayfarer. The wayfarer is tossed and turned between his instinctual need to obey the demands of his ego and its will-to-control, and his aspiration to transcend the limitations of the ego.

What Tweedie documented for her readers is the process of the gradual grinding down of her ego. This was the nature of the training she had undergone with Bhai Sahib, and in this her teacher followed in the footsteps of countless teachers before him. The grinding down of the wilful ego is a prerequisite for the emergence of the pure light contained within the Heart of Hearts. And it is done through love.

> Two days before he left he was explaining a bit about his seeming rudeness. 'If one chooses the Way of Love, it does not take long, relatively. But it is difficult. Life becomes very sad. No joy. Thorns everywhere. This has to be crossed. Then all of a sudden there will be flowers and sunshine. But the road has to be crossed first. There is nothing which can be done about it. People will hear one day that you have been turned out; and not only that, but other things too. And it is not the disciple who chooses which road to take; it is the teacher who decides. There are two roads: The road of Dhyana, the slow one, and the road of *Tyaga*, of complete renunciation, of Surrender: this is the Direct Road, the Path of Fire, the Path of Love' (Tweedie 1986:237).
>
> Even on the worldly platform it works in a similar way. If one is much in love, the lover is forgetful of everything else except the object of his love. He is distraught; people call him mad. The law is the same on all the levels of being. Only on the spiritual level the law is more powerful because there are no obstructions caused by the density of matter. After a moment of silence he added with one of his flashing smiles: 'We are called the fools, the idiots of God, by the Sufi poets' (1986:236).

The density of matter and the frailty of the human body become part of the process of transformation through the grinding down of the ego. *Daughter of Fire* is among other things a documentation of the physical suffering on the path of transformation. The body suffers because it is almost beyond its capacity to contain the emotional intensity stirred up by the many-faceted experiences of love. The teacher produced this ever-growing intensity by revealing to the disciple, through his attitude and behaviour towards her, the two complementary, yet opposing, Divine attributes of Mercy/Beauty and Power/Majesty. [13]

> 'According to the system the *shishya* [disciple] is constantly kept between the opposites, ups and downs; it creates the friction necessary to cause suffering which will defeat the mind. The greatest obstacle on the spiritual path is to make people understand that they have to give up everything' (1986:187).

The disciple experiences the teacher as benevolent, compassionate, tender, radiant with unearthly beauty. Then, in a flash, the teacher reveals his other face: he is strict, demanding, devastating, tyrannical, rejecting. We read such descriptions in the old manuals, and we read it also in Tweedie's documentation. Rumi says: You are bewildered by my severity; I am mighty severe, but there are a thousand gentlenesses in my severity. [14]

On 11th August 1961 Tweedie writes:

> This morning I felt very bad ... vomiting condition, and severe headache ... Went there about nine. He was not outside ... I felt so hot; the night was stifling hot. Felt miserable. Not a leaf was stirring in the trees ... He came in after his bath ... He was talking and laughing with his wife. When the wife had left, I told him how I suffered last night ... 'You should not sit here for hours', he interrupted me sharply. 'It won't help you. The mind is not working; you are apt to criticize; unnecessary questions arise in your mind which you may think helpful, but they are not; they are the worst kind! You come here from nine to ten, for one hour in the morning, and then in the evening for a short time'. I began to weep. 'You are sending me away into the heat! How cruel! You know that my flat is as hot as a baker's oven – the coolest place is this room of yours under the fan ... I am here to be with you ... I understood that is how it should be'.
> 'To be with me', he repeated scornfully ... 'Others are with me too. My wife, my children ... they serve me! But you, what are you doing?' (1986:255).

The teacher thus, intentionally, creates this terrible friction, the feeling of tremendous isolation, loneliness, separation, rejection. Many Sufi writings describe such states.

These are descriptions of the dark night of the soul. Without the descent into the deepest despair, one cannot overcome one's fear – the existential fear of losing one's sense of security, confidence, even one's identity, past, present, future. It is against the background of this wretched sense of isolation and separation that the disciple becomes aware of – indeed, is overtaken by – deep and hopeless longing. But it is this longing which ultimately creates the vacuum, the emptiness, into which the Divine can enter.

On 21st August Tweedie writes:

> Yes ... The longing ... the Great ... the Endless ... I was just waking up ... and there it was ... the Longing ... so great, so endless, and oh, so sharply painful, and so deep ... Longing for what? ... I really did not know. I never do. Since I am here with Bhai Sahib it is just longing ... sometimes like a deep sigh from the bottom of my heart ... or I had to cry out loudly ... it was so sharp, so cruel ... Confused, tortured, the mind not working ... it was just longing from the very depth of the heart, the poignant feeling of some vanished bliss ... This morning ... it was the same as I always knew, only stronger, more positive, more definite. For a few seconds it seemed to be breaking my body apart, so strong it was, causing even bodily pain. Then it ebbed away, leaving the understanding of its very nature behind. So simple: all the time it was never anything else but THE CRY FOR THE REAL HOME! (1986:263).

Soon after this experience, on 22nd August, Tweedie records tender words, full of promise and consolation, coming from her teacher:

> 'If you write the book do not forget to emphasize how love is created ... My disciples, if they live as I expect them to live, and they follow me in everything, they realize God IN THIS LIFE. Absolutely ... God MUST be realized in one life, in this life ... After a few years you will say: to what a wonderful system you have been attracted ... I am scolding you because I know that love is greater than anything. My Rev. Guru Maharaj kept scolding me, and I just sat there with my head bent. I kept thinking that he is right, and I am a fool to rebel all the time. He never scolded anybody else as much as he did me' (1986:266).

This, then, is the story of a training. But it is also a documentation of the way in which the esoteric tradition is transmitted and perpetuated. All Sufi fraternities and Paths faithfully record their particular chain of transmission from teacher to disciple *(silsila* – see above), generation by generation. Recording the teacher-disciple relationship is therefore also the recording of a link, or rather a double link, in the chain of a mystical system. This in mind, I would like to end with Tweedie's words from the last entry in her diary. On 9th March 1967, before returning from her Himalayan retreat to England, she wrote:

> I remember that after your death I felt like screaming only at the thought of returning to the West. Could not reconcile the states of oneness and the world around me. Solitude was the only way out. To be able to find myself again, which was not a self at all. I know now, that I can never be alone anymore, for you are with me always. I know that God is Silence and can be reached only in silence. I will try to help people to reach this state, this is a promise, and I will keep it (1986:819).

Notes

1.   Both presentations rely heavily on two fifteenth-century Persian sources: *Rashahat 'ain al-hayat* ('Dew-drops from the Spring of Life'), by al-Kashifi, and *Nafahat al-' uns* ('Breaths of Divine Intimacy') by al-Jami (d.1492).

2.   For a list of the eleven principles of the *naqshbandiyya* see Trimingham (1971:203-4).

3.   On the practice of *dhikr* (remembrance of God) in the Sufi tradition in general, see Schimmel (1975:167ff); Nicholson (1963:45ff); Andrae (1987:82ff); Trimingham (1971:194ff).

4.   On the *sama* and the practice of reciting or listening to scriptural passages, music and poetry, especially love poetry, see Schimmel (1975:178-86); Trimingham (1971:200ff).

5.   The following anecdote is related by al-Hujwiri, an eleventh-century Sufi author, in his *Kashf al-Mahjub* ('The Unveiling of the Veiled'), one of the classics of Sufi literature. 'A certain man says, I was walking on a mountain road with Ibrahim Khawwas [a ninth-century Sufi from Iraq]. A sudden thrill of emotion seized my heart, and I chanted: "All men are sure that I am in love. But they know not whom I love..." Ibrahim begged me to repeat the verses, and I did so. In sympathetic ecstasy he danced a few steps on the stony ground. I observed that his feet sank into the rock as though it were wax. Then he fell in a swoon. On coming to himself he said to me: I have been in Paradise, and you were unaware.' Nicholson (1976:410).

6.   Tweedie: 'The colour of our Line is golden yellow, and we are called the Golden Sufis or the Silent Sufis, because we practice silent meditation. We do not use music or dancing or any definite practice. We do not belong to any country or any civilization, but we work always according to the need of the people of the time' (1986:20).

7.   For more on the silent *dhikr* and the role of Baha' al-Din Naqshband in re-instituting this practice, see ter Haar (1992:316ff).

8.   This title reflects the image of Sirhindi as a religious reformer at the beginning of the second Islamic millennium. (The year 622 C.E. corresponds to the year 1 H. [*Hijra*] in Muslim chronology. On his personality and teaching see Friedmann (1971).

9.   Cf. the concept of *qabbalah* (Hebrew transmitted tradition) in Jewish mysticism. See e.g. Scholem (1961:20-21).

10.   See Ibn 'Arabi in Chittick (1989:108).

11.   Much has been written about Jalal al-Din Rumi, his poetry, and his relationship with his spiritual guide Shams-i Tabriz-i. See, e.g., Chittick 1983 and the Selected Bibliography and Index of Sources, 375-95.

12.   On the polar opposites *fanaa wa-baqaa* (annihilation and subsistence) in the Sufi tradition see, e.g., Schimmel (1975:142ff); Sviri (1987:316-49); Arberry (1977, ch.59, p.120-32; Chittick (1983:179-81); and cf.. the following quotation from Ibn 'Arabi: 'Through being joined to the Real, man is annihilated from himself. Then the Real becomes manifest so that He is his hearing and his sight' (cited in Chittick (1983:328).

13.   On the polar Divine attributes *jamal* (beauty) and *jalal* (majesty), see Murata (1992, esp. 69ff); Sviri (1987).

14.   Cf. also the following verses by Rumi, quoted in Chittick (1983:p.227):

> Sometimes He shows Himself in one way,
> Sometimes in the opposite way –
> the work of religion is naught but bewilderment ...
> Once you have become bewildered, dizzy and annihilated,
> then your spiritual state will say 'Lead us on the Straight Path!'
> Severity is truly awesome, but once you begin to tremble, that awesomeness
> becomes soft and smoot

References

Tor Andre (1987) *In the Garden of Myrtles: Studies in Early Islamic Mysticism*, New York: SUNY Press

A J Arberry (ed.) (1947) *K. al-riyada wa-adab al-nafs*, Cairo

A J Arberry (1977) *The Doctrine of the Sufis*, Cambridge: Cambridge University Press (translated from the Arabic of Abu Bakr al-Kalabadhi)

J G Bennett (1977) *The Masters of Wisdom*, Wellingborough: Turnstone

William C Chittick (1983) *The Sufi Path of Love*, New York: State University of New York Press

William C Chittick (1989) *The Sufi Path of Knowledge*, Albany: SUNY Press

Y Friedmann (1971) *Shaykh Ahmad Sirhindi*, Montreal: McGill-Queen's University Press

G J ter Haar (1992) The importance of the Spiritual Guide in the Naqshbandi Order, in *The Legacy of Mediaeval Sufism*, ed. L. Lewisohn, London: Khaniqahi Nimatullahi Publications in association with the SOAS Centre of Near and Middle Eastern Studies

Sachiko Murata (1992) *The Tao of Islam: A Sourcebook on Gender Relationship in Islamic Thought*, New York: State University of New York Press

R A Nicholson (1963) *The Mystics of Islam*, London: Luzac & Co.

R A Nicholson (tr.) (1976) *Kashf al-Mahjub*, London: Luzac & Co.

A Schimmel (1975) Mystical Dimensions of Islam, University of North Carolina Press

G Scholem (1961) *Major Trends in Jewish Mysticism*, New York: Schocken Books

Hasan Shushud (1983) *Masters of Wisdom of Central Asia*, Coombe Springs Press

S Sviri (1987) Between fear and hope: on the coincidence of opposites in Islamic mysticism, *Jerusalem Studies in Arabic and Islam*, 9, 316-49

S Sviri 'Does God pray? A Judaeo-Islamic tradition in the light of analytical psychology, *European Judaism*, 25(48), 48-55

J S Trimingham (1971) *The Sufi Orders in Islam*, Oxford: Oxford University Press

Irina Tweedie (1978) *The Chasm of Fire*, Shaftesbury: Element

Irina Tweedie (1986) *Daughter of Fire*, Nevada City: Blue Dolphin Publications

7

Women disciples in Zen Buddhism

ANNE BANCROFT

The spiritual lineage of Zen is called the patriarchal line. A twelfth-century Zen master in Japan stressed that 'Nuns, women or evil people should on no account be permitted to stay overnight' in a monastery, and certainly until quite recently the general attitude towards religious women reflected the sexist attitude of the entire culture in Eastern countries.

Only in the post-war era have Japanese Zen nuns been allowed to ordain disciples or serve as head priests of temples. There are two main schools in Zen, Soto and Rinzai, and Soto is considerably the bigger. After a long struggle, Soto nuns first won the right to ordain disciples and give Dharma transmission in 1951, and since 1970 they have been allowed to serve as the head priests of low-ranking branch temples. Discrimination still shows itself, however, in that women priests are not allowed to marry, while men are.

In 1984, in Soto Zen in Japan, there were 177 female clergy to 15,528 males.

The roshi-student relationship

Discipleship in Japanese Zen Buddhism takes the form of joining a monastery for Zen training which will be under a Zen master called a roshi. The only women roshis that I am aware of are Westerners living in America. The disciple is expected to follow a daily routine of meditation, chanting and physical work for a number of years. There is some contact with the roshi, listening to his talks and having interviews. Essentially the disciple is expected to do whatever he or she is told to by the roshi and by the hierarchy of the monastery. The seniority system in Japan still affects nearly all aspects of monastic life. If one monk arrives in the morning and another arrives that afternoon, the afternoon one has to defer to the morning one for the rest of their monastic career.

However, although trust in the roshi and trust in the system is an essential basis for the roshi-student relationship and for the deepening of the practice, it does not have to be a blind trust. If the relationship does not work out, the disciple can go elsewhere.

Part of the problem of transferring Zen to the West – and I now want to look at the discipleship position in America, where a number of Japanese roshis have settled – is that the roshi-disciple relationship is not always understood. Individuals and groups, even normally sceptical people, sometimes invest the roshi with an almost divine aura. Disillusionment follows when the roshi turns out to be all too human, with a drink or womanizing problem. Women in particular have suffered from expectations of celibacy in their teachers, only to have those expectations shattered by an amorous advance.

The growth of Zen in the West

The most significant new feature of Zen is its growth in the West, probably now equalling that of Japan. And the most important feature of that growth is the full participation of women. Men and women sit together as lay disciples in the meditation hall, and women are in positions of influence at all the major Zen centres. With the importance of their role they now challenge the old patterns of hierarchy. Joanna Macy, one of the foremost American Buddhists, now sees the role of women as pivotal in the future development of not only Zen but all Buddhism. She says:

> As American women opening to the Dharma, we are participating in something beyond our own little scenarios. We find ourselves reclaiming the equality of the sexes in the Buddha Dharma. We are participating in a balancing of Buddhism that has great historic significance ... I see Buddhism as a tradition that has suffered under several thousand years of patriarchy. Now there is a return, and we can see more clearly the male-dominated, hierarchical patterns that have arisen in the last two millennia ... We do not have to buy into hierarchical understandings of what power is, because the central teaching of the Buddha himself – the vision of dependent

co-arising – shows that power is essentially relational and reciprocal (The Balancing of American Buddhism, 1986).

Macy links the equality of the sexes to the structure of power, a real challenge to the old order. With the emergence of women head teachers and roshis, the whole feeling of Zen must inevitably change. It has yet to be played out.

The other great difference between Western and Eastern Zen is the development in the West of a strong lay movement rather than a monastic one. Indeed, as Kenneth Kraft points out, if Western Zen cannot survive as a lay practice it may not survive at all. Thus there is a continuing struggle going on to establish Zen as a lifetime religious way rather than as a narrowly goal-orientated practice. Japanese Zen emphasizes the vertical relationship whereby a monk is supposed to be loyal to the person above and responsible for the person below, but in the West the wish for democratic lay organizations is changing that concept.

Women are at the forefront in this change, for if Zen is to be a lifetime way for lay people it is essential that they take part. This can be hard. One of them says:

> We have a tremendous yearning to take the spiritual search all the way to the bottom, to put aside all the things that restrict and bind us and keep us from pursuing that search full-time. To do that, we have to do zazen. We have to do retreats, set aside hours, days, weeks, to pursue that search. Meanwhile, what are we leaving at home? Jobs, housework, children. As we sit in meditation visions of spiritual orphans float through our heads. We picture our child, wandering through the neighbourhood, dirty in an unironed shirt, thumb in his mouth. Someone says, 'Where's your mummy?' 'My mummy is getting enlightened' (*Kahawai* 1984:35).

There are still many anomalies in the Western Zen scene. There are splits and scandals and centres which disintegrate. But it is beginning to appear that Zen can survive, especially if a Westerner has become an ordained roshi. Indeed, some Western roshis, both men and women, have given Zen new meaning and new life and yet kept the essential teaching as the vital ingredient.

Sexual misconduct and the abuse of power
There still remains, however, the conceptual difference between West and East with regard to the teacher-disciple relationship, and this is most apparent in the field of sexual misconduct and the abuse of power. A number of American women have spoken out on this subject. One is a woman roshi, Maurine Stuart. When one of her

94

Japanese teachers was found to be making advances to a number of his students, she
said: 'I felt that everyone in the sangha had been betrayed. I wasn't judgemental about
sex, or about a teacher having sex with a student, but in this situation it was an unloving
act. It was the misuse of sex and of women and the manipulations that were so
devastating' (*Kahawai* 1984).

In communities that have lived through disruptive teacher-student relationships,
members tend to agree that while sex itself has not been the key issue, it throws into
relief the question of moral authority. Sexual harassment is essentially an issue of
power, and spiritual teachers often enjoy an unusual amount of uncontested power
because of the hierarchical organizational structures adopted from the East. These
hierarchical forms reflect the values of the feudal system of class division and of
authoritarian control under which most spiritual traditions were founded, rather than
modern values of democracy. So it looks as though the two great issues of female
participation and of lay democracy are going to change the face of Zen, perhaps for
good. Katy Butler, a member of the San Francisco Zen Center, says:

> For a long time most of us accepted without thinking it through, foreign
> conceptions of hierarchy, of information restricted on a 'need to know'
> basis. Coming from a culture almost devoid of ways of showing respect,
> some of us hungrily took on another way. Now these foreign ideas are being
> tested for their usefulness against the genius of western culture: democracy,
> open information, a free press, psychological development, the separation
> of Church and State, and a system of checks and balances' (*Kahawai*
> 1984:7)

At an American symposium on women and Buddhism in 1983 a great deal was said
on the abuse of power by teachers. One woman asked:

> What was it in me that chose someone and gave power to someone who
> would abuse me in some way? What was it in my and that other person's
> conditioning that puts us together in a place where we would use each other
> in that way?
> It's true that if someone is a teacher, you have a right to expect them to
> be more responsible than you, to know more than you. Nevertheless, I have
> observed in myself a willingness to absolve myself of responsibilities, a
> willingness to believe that this person is something bigger than human. I've
> had to re-examine what is a master and what do I want from a master.
> Although one has a right to expect (to put it mildly) good behaviour from
> a master, in places where there was someone to whom I have given power,
> I have given up responsibility for what happens in that relationship.
> It is give and take with a teacher and no matter how badly I've been hurt,
> every time I've had a bad experience, I've learned. That's part of what

happens with growing up and with any relationship. You get hurt and then you learn and come to terms with the ways in which you were responsible for a part of what happened. It doesn't just happen with Dharma teachers or just with women. It happens to men too. I know a lot of men who have been deeply hurt in relationships with Dharma teachers.

This kind of abuse happens when there is someone to whom a lot of power is given and someone who doesn't take responsibility. Male-female relationships, relationships with Dharma teachers, are ripe for that because of our long-term conditioning in which men have more power and are taught to use it, and women are taught to give in to it. Nonetheless, that person is a victim of the same conditioning and on some level is being hurt by what they're doing (*Kahawai* 1984:15).

There is an admirable frankness among American women. It has borne fruit in some Zen communities where the teacher is now supported by a number of disciples who also teach and where the construction of the community is entirely democratic and often family-based. Disciples with their families form the major part of such a community and the children have an active role in all that is done. One example is the San Francisco Zen Center where the roshi is a man called Reb Anderson, who himself is married and has a child. Another is the Providence Zen Center of Rhode Island, with a Korean roshi, where many of the members live with their families in houses on what one might call the campus.

The problems of Zen discipleship for women and also the rewards will continue for many years to play their part in the development of Western Zen. But such problems may well be solved by the questioning spirit which is itself part of the Zen tradition. It is also the spirit which attracts women to Zen in the first place (Who am I? What does it mean to be a human being? What is the purpose of life and death?) This same element of doubt brings them to query the language and customs of tradition and of sex-role stereotypes in leadership. The spirit of women's practice is becoming infused with a feminist consciousness, one which brings down the barriers between the sexes in order that men and women can share the practice together on equal terms.

References

'The Balancing of American Buddhism' Primary Point, (February 1986) 3(1), 6, (transcription slightly modified)

Lenore Friedman (1987) *Meetings with Remarkable Women*, Boston: Shambala

A Gathering of Spirit: Women Teaching on American Buddhism, Primary Point Press (1985)

Kahawai: Journal of Women and Zen (Spring 1984), 6(2)

Kenneth Kraft (ed.) (1988) *Zen: Tradition and Transition*, New York: Grove Press

Helen Tworkov (1989) *Zen in America*, California

8

Why women are priests and teachers in Bahian Candomble

PETER B. CLARKE

During my research carried out annually from 1986-91 I was struck by the large number of women priests in Candomble in Bahia in north-eastern Brazil. Other researchers, most notably the American anthropologist Ruth Landes (1947) and the French anthropologist Gisèle Cossard-Binon (1974) were also surprised by the very great number of priestesses in this part of Brazil, and as will be seen below the former offered a detailed gender-based explanation for this phenomenon. These priestesses are referred to either by their Yoruba title *iyalorisha*, mother of the god, or by the Portuguese term mae-de-santo, which means mother of the saint or holy one or divinity. In rituals where possession is the climax the mediums are mounted (Yoruba: gun) by African, mainly Yoruba, gods (Yoruba:orisa; Portuguese:orixa) and become their horses (cavalos).

As will be seen below, the reasons for the prominence of women in Candomble in Bahia are, in the light of modern thinking on gender and the role of women in society, both positive and negative. On the one hand, in the popular mind women leaders are, in contrast with men, calm, rational, logical and in control of their emotions, all traditionally regarded as male attributes, while on the other hand they provide the most appropriate symbols of the correct relationship – that of subordination and service – between a devotee and a god, all of whom are in a sense regarded as male.

The situation is different elsewhere, for example further north in the state of Pernambuco where Candomble is known by the name of the Yoruba God of thunder, Xango (Yoruba: Sango). There, men are very often the leaders or priests and mediums – known by the Yoruba designation of *babalorisha*, father of the god, or in Portuguese as pais-de-santo, fathers of the saint and/or holy one.

In most respects Candomble (Afro-Brazilian religion as practised in Bahia) bears a very close resemblance to Pernambucan Xango. However, it differs considerably from Umbanda which is much more widely practised in Rio de Janeiro, Sao Paulo and the south of Brazil generally. Umbanda, like Candomble, varies both in form and content from one centre or terreiro to another. Nevertheless, it is true to say that Umbanda has on the whole absorbed many more non-African elements, such as the Spiritism of Kardec (Hess 1991:15), than Candomble. Indeed, Candomble terreiros have, it would appear, deliberately attempted to keep themselves free from such influence.

Candomble in Bahia comes in two basic forms: firstly Nago, also known as Yoruba from its close links with the Yoruba culture of western Africa. The main concern here is with this Yoruba-based Candomble, the most widespread form today in Bahia which will be referred to simply as Nago, a word used mainly in Bahia and in the Republic of Benin in west Africa for the Yoruba (da Costa Lima 1984: 7-9). The other main form of Candomble is Angolan, which was shaped historically by the beliefs and practices of the slaves from west-central, south-eastern and southern Africa. Today it contains a large Amerindian or Caboclo element. It is worth noting that there are a number of sub-divisions of Nago Candomble, including Ketu, which derives from the old Yoruba town of Ketu situated in the present-day Republic of Benin in western Africa, and Jeje which originates from the Fon, also of the Republic of Benin. Although the differences between the various forms of Candomble are often small they can be of considerable importance to members (de Costa Lima 1984:18). One example of a difference is to be found in the way the music is played: while one tradition, the Nago, will use drum sticks to beat the drums that call upon the gods from Africa to possess their daughters and sons, another, the Angolan, will make use simply of the hands for the same purpose.

Each tradition has incorporated elements from the others and each one has in varying degrees accepted elements of indigenous Amerindian belief and ritual (de Costa Lima 1984: 10-26). However, more Amerindian ritual and belief is found in

Angolan-based Candomble than in the western African forms. Also, more use is made of the Portuguese language in Angolan Candomble than in the other traditions. All of these traditions have many Catholic elements and equate their African gods and indigenous Amerindian spirits (caboclos) with Catholic saints, a practice also found in Cuban Santeria, Haitian Voodoo and elsewhere in Central, North and South America where African religion and Catholicism have met. For example, the Yoruba god of thunder, Xango, already mentioned, is equated in Bahia with St Jerome.

Some researchers, among them Valente (1977), describe the relationship between Candomble and Catholicism as syncretistic, while others, including Verger (Verger Interviews: 1986-91), speak not of the blending or mixing of the two faiths but of the way they are kept separate by believers, using the term 'juxtapositioning' to describe this. Most members of Candomble are Catholics, and some clearly make a very definite separation, sometimes conveyed symbolically to participants at a Candomble ceremony, between the two religions. For example, a medium before entering trance will have the crucifix which she is wearing round her neck removed. However, for many people Catholicism and Candomble are seen as little more than different expressions – African and European – of the same spiritual reality (Olga Francisca Regis 1984:27-35). To the candomblesista of African descent the spiritual world is seen as one world and religions as different ways, culturally determined, of expressing and conveying to people the power of that world.

Cultural identity offers another reason for syncretism. There are few if any members of Candomble who can claim to be entirely of African descent. Most will have some Amerindian or European ancestry and this in itself makes it virtually impossible to insist on any rigid separation between the various religious traditions found in Bahia. To do so would mean for many to cut themselves off from a part of their personal history which they are seeking to reconstruct through Candomble. Although, as already noted, the various traditions of Candomble have changed over time through interaction with each other and with both indigenous Amerindian religious beliefs and practices and Catholicism, the Nago tradition, which is the most widely practised in Bahia, has remained closest to its African roots (Bastide: 1960).

In Salvador, the capital city of the state of Bahia, there are an estimated two thousand terreiros or compounds, varying in size from as few as twenty devotees to hundreds. Some are old, well endowed, and exercise a great deal of influence in the political sphere, while others resemble the base communities of Liberation Theology and have little or no influence on the wider society, but can be highly effective at the grass-roots level. All are affected by the present harsh economic climate, including the gods who are obliged to accept in the form of a sacrifice not only less but also poorer quality food. Moreover, economic hardship makes it extremely difficult to continue with many of the traditional rules and regulations governing the rite of initiation such as the seclusion of novices for a set period of time, and the purchase of those items necessary for the initiation ceremony itself. Subsequent rites that mark the stages in the ascent of the devotee to the office of priest are also affected in this way.

Generally a Candomble ceremony will begin with the sacrifice of an animal – a cock, goat or pigeon – performed by the sacrificer to the sound of the drums. Where possible the sacrificer is a man. He is assisted by other males and from among the women members by the mae-de-santo alone. There are instances, as Herskovits (1943) noted long ago in Porto Alegre, where the sacrifice is performed by women. I have also observed in my own research women performing the sacrifice, especially in the very poor centres of worship. On these occasions other women who had abstained from sexual intercourse during the previous 24 hours were permitted to attend. Also to be noted is that sacrifice can take a variety of forms other than animal sacrifice. At times it will consist of an elaborate iced cake resembling a huge wedding cake made and offered by the women members. Nevertheless, normally only men are regarded as legitimate sacrificers principally for the reason that impure menstrual blood would render the sacrifice ineffective.

Occasionally very different reasons are given by the maes-de-santo and their disciples for male sacrificers. One informant, a revered mae-de-santo, dismissed any ideas that impure menstrual blood would invalidate the sacrifice and pointed out that it was simply because the sacrificial victim could be large and powerful – a cow or a pig – that it was preferable for a man who was physically stronger than a woman to perform this role. Although sacrifice of some kind is necessary for the ceremony to be complete, at the centre of the Candomble experience is possession. The gods are called upon by means of drumming and chanting, as previously pointed out, to incorporate in their devotees.

In the Yoruba context in south-western Nigeria and the Republic of Benin where most of them have their origin, many of the gods or orisa are best described as 'forces of nature'. They have a nature aspect to their make-up, associated as they are in the popular mind with various features of the local environment such as rivers, rocks, hills, mineral deposits and storm winds. However, some, such as the god of thunder Xango (Sango) already mentioned, also have what Horton terms a 'deified hero' aspect to their being in that they are thought of as:

> the spiritual residues of great men or women of earlier times who vanished into the sky, water, earth or mountain instead of undergoing normal death or burial.
> As such, they are credited with highly distinctive and individual personalities (1983:61).

The orisa or gods not only bring prosperity to the community in return for proper attention but also play a crucial role in the life of the individual by enabling the latter, in return for regular propitiatory offerings, daily salutations and memorial rites recalling their exploits, to either realize the good destiny which s/he chose before birth or to mitigate the negative consequences of a bad choice. Devotees each have as guardian and protector a god and his consort whom they resemble closely in character and who enables them to fulfil their destiny. Destiny is not fixed to the letter but can be modified, though not fundamentally altered.

This interdependence between devotee and god can become so intense that the former will eventually be possessed by their god, usually at a festival, and come to take on his character. Their god's personality will become the model according to which devotees will assess their own worth, potential and appeal, and regulate their conduct and relationships with others. Often a devotee will act out the behaviour characteristic of her/his god; thus one dedicated to the god of iron, Ogun, will display a very mixed set of characteristics which at one and the same time attract and repel: irascibility, unpredictability, openness and generosity.

The gods are also the embodiment and bearers of *ase*, perhaps the most important notion in Yoruba religion and defined by Thompson as 'the power to make things happen', or as 'God's own enabling light rendered accessible to men and women' (1984: 5). Olorun (Lord of the heavens), the supreme deity, is neither male nor female but a vital force, the quintessential form of *ase* which is released through the orisa in keeping with their character. Besides the gods, trees such as the iroko tree, and substances such as iron, blood and semen can be vehicles for the transmission of *ase*, most potent when acquired through possession.

In Brazil not all who are possessed either desire or enjoy the experience. Few will try to explain what happens and many will describe its effects quite simply as making them feel lighter (*mais leve*), refreshed, renewed. What one sees by way of response on the part of the devotee when a god incorporates is teleguided by the iyalorisha (chief priestess) or the babalorisha (chief priest).

Initiation is not a sine qua non of possession; the one possessed can be a young child or a person with no formal links with a terreiro. Moreover, possession can occur quite randomly. For example while a person is carrying out such routine tasks as cooking or washing or cleaning the shrine of a god. In this kind of setting possession is often a means of maintaining order and discipline in a terreiro, for the one so possessed is usually entrusted with a message for the leadership concerning a misdemeanour or a potential source of conflict within the community.

The main question here, however, is not the mechanics or purpose of possession but why the priests are so often women. We can begin our search for an explanation of this phenomenon by turning to the research carried out by the anthropologist Ruth Landes.

Landes, gender and the preponderance of women priests

Landes, who carried out her research some fifty years ago, explained the large number of women priests in Salvador largely in terms of gender. She also gave a certain weight – though not nearly enough – to economic and historical factors. Landes was not alone in believing that it was 'unnatural' for men to be priests in Candomble. At the funeral of the widely revered Mae de Santo Aninha, she asked Edison Carneiro, an authority on Candomble, if it were not unusual for women in Brazil to receive the high level of recognition such as this priestess had been given, and his reply was:

> Not in Bahia ... Not in the world of Candomble. The shoe is on the other foot here. It is almost as difficult for a man to become great in Candomble as it is for him to have a baby. And for the same reason: it is believed to be against his nature. (Ibid)

Space permits only the very briefest of summaries of Landes's theory here. The thrust of her main argument is that women alone are by nature capable of that inner contemplation and spiritual experience that participation in Candomble requires. They alone, furthermore, are able to receive, comprehend and express the central message of Candomble which is mediated through dance. She writes:

> Dance to them (members of Candomble) is life. It is their avenue of comprehension and response and their way of thinking, their manner of expressing themselves. (1947: 224)

Landes then goes on to assert that where women are concerned the effects of dance are normal while men, in contrast, are incapable of experiencing these effects while normal. After observing one of the devotees move from dance to trance, urged on by drumming and clapping, Landes wrote:

> Elizabeth of Xango (Yoruba god of thunder) appeared to be in love with herself, and after, when the divinity had incorporated in her, it was as if she was dominated by an intense passion. Her life at that moment rose to its deepest, most profound significance. It is a pity men are not capable of that experience except when abnormal ... and the reason is they are considered (by members of Candomble and in wider society) to be of earthy material and the best they can do is to dance in the streets. (1947: 224)

In the opinion of the local people, Landes informs us, men are incapable of that deep spiritual experience brought on by dance because they are, 'hot, excited, profane and mundane'. Informants told her:

> The spirit of man is always on roads and does not return to within himself where it could serve as an instrument of the gods. (ibid)

There was, however, an exception to this rule in the person of the male homosexual, more precisely in the passive male homosexual. Landes writes of one well known babalorisha allegedly of this tendency,

> I believe that he is sufficiently honest about the practices of the cult to wish he were indeed a woman. Being a man he has to delegate many of the crucial functions to a woman member of the cult and in the last resort it is she who counts not him. (ibid: 227)

Male priests in Candomble were, in Landes's opinion, a sexual anomaly. It was only by virtue of their femininity that passive homosexuals were able to perform the role of medium in anything like an authentic manner. In effect the only truly valid priest and medium was a woman on the grounds of her natural innate disposition qua woman to express in dance that deep inner awareness of the self as divine and to act as a channel for the communication of the spiritual, sacred, transcendent form of life to others.

Landes' main critics

Several scholars have dismissed as groundless Landes's basic premise that women are by nature more suited to the role of priest than men. The French sociologist Bastide wrote of her 'biased', 'lopsided' and

> female view of Candomble that reflects the spirit of female protest in the United States which all observers have seen as a fundamental characteristic of that country (1960: 307).

In reply to Bastide's objection it is worth pointing out first of all that one of Landes's main sources on the feminist dimension to Candomble was the Brazilian professor of law Senhor Duarte, and not the American feminist movement. Duarte wrote of the immense difficulties women experienced in obtaining equality of treatment with men in religion or in any other sphere of life in a predominantly patriarchal society such as Brazil (Landes 1947: 86).

Bastide did point out quite correctly that in Brazil, the Caribbean, and Africa from where it originated, Candomble and its equivalents were largely in the hands of men. Verger makes the same point in his own refutation of Landes's theory (1985). This line of argument seriously undermines Landes's thesis, although it is undeniably the case that the majority of priests in Bahian Candomble are women. Verger maintains that this can be accounted for solely in terms of economics, history and tradition and reminds his readers that all devotees are in a sense female, recalling that after his own initiation ceremony had been completed he was informed by the officiating priestess that he should now consider himself to be the *wife* of his god, Xango. This, Verger insists, had nothing to do with either his or his deity's sexual orientation, but simply provided the most apt model of the kind of relationship that should exist between a devotee and her/his god (Verger Interviews:1986-91).

For the sake of completeness and by way of response to Verger's critique of her thesis, the point needs to be made that Landes also, as previously mentioned, spoke of the importance of history and economics in the development of a female priesthood in Bahia. The main historical reason given by her is that during the era of the slave trade women as domestic slaves came to occupy a more prominent and responsible position in what was left of the African family. Women functioned as family heads residing in the Casa Grande or the slave owner's compound and close to their children, while their husbands were confined for the most part to the plantations. They also became the mediators between the slave masters and the male slaves and came to be appreciated as effective and skilful negotiators and conciliators, qualities of the utmost importance for the successful running of a roca or Candomble compound. Furthermore, women slaves, Landes maintains, had better access to markets and therefore more opportunity to advance economically and purchase their freedom than men.

To return to Verger and the prominence of women in Candomble. He rightly attaches considerably more importance than Landes to African tradition and in particular to the tradition of *Iyanaso* in the construction of Candomble in Bahia and the prominent role of women therein. However, Brazilianized Candomble continues to feed off things African especially African traditions. Indeed, African religion as found among the Yoruba of south-western Nigeria and the Republic of Benin constitutes something of a sacred text for much of Nago Candomble in Bahia, albeit a text that can be adapted and changed when necessary. This is the conceptual framework in which the *Iyanoso* tradition in Brazil needs to be interpreted.

The meaning of the title *Iyanaso* has been discussed at some length by da Costa Lima among others (1984: 23). In west Africa it denoted a religious role involving responsibility for the worship of the personal deity of the King and/or Alafin of the Yoruba empire, Xango (Yoruba:Sango). The *Iyanaso*, one of the eight priestesses in the royal household, had the dubious privilege of being one of the four priestesses to accompany the king into the afterlife by committing suicide on his death.

The relevance of this tradition to the development of Candomble in Bahia and the predominance of women priests there lies in the fact that the foundress of the oldest Candomble terreiro in Bahia, established in the early 1820s, the Casa Branca (White House), bore the title of *Iyanaso*. It is also very likely that this centre provided a model for other Candomble terreiros in the capital city of Bahia, Salvador. In fact, some of the more historic, better known and highly influential centres such as the Gantois terreiro, made famous by the late Mae Menininha (d.1986), were offshoots of the Casa Branca and looked to it as the model. My own research suggests that there are several other important reasons, some of which indicate an extremely traditional and ambivalent view of the role of women in society, as to why women are the priests and teachers in Candomble. Indeed, they could be said to be the priests because they possess attributes largely thought of as male to a higher degree than most men.

Moreover, as will be seen, the female is seen as symbolic of the ideal devotee.

However, this is only part of the explanation. The early priestesses were undoubtedly charismatic in the Weberian understanding of that term and they and their successors owed and still owe much of their authority to their dynamism and moral standing and their knowledge of the inner secrets of the religion. We will begin our own assessment of their position with this last point.

Living archives

Candomble is largely based on oral tradition, and the position of women is enhanced by virtue of the fact that they established for themselves a reputation as extremely reliable sources of information about the myths, rituals and cures that give Candomble its shape, substance and value. Women are sometimes referred to as Candomble's 'Living Archives'. One of the more widely known of Yoruba myths in Bahia, now heavily Brazilianized, reveals that from the very beginning men and women have been locked in a power struggle, and sees 'secret knowledge' as the principal weapon in this war of the sexes. It bears the title *How Men Came to Dominate Women* and is worth quoting at some length:

> At the beginning of the world women intimidated the men of that time. It was Yansan (goddess of fresh water) who first invented the secrets of freemasonry ... When women wanted to enslave their husbands they came together at the crossroads with Yansan in front. One day the men deliberated over how to end such shame and embarrassment. The babalawo (diviner) sent the male divinity Ogun (the god of iron) to make a sacrifice, to dress in a large dressing gown (for the purpose of disguise) and to carry in his hand a large sword. This Ogun did on that day when all the women were gathered together to celebrate a customary feast ... Ogun suddenly appeared among the women as a terrifying old man and Yansan, the leader of women, became known to all and sundry. As a result she disappeared forever from the earth. It was in this way that men came to dominate women and to this day they do not allow them knowledge of the secrets whatever they may be, unless it be question of a very exceptional woman (my trans from:Braga, 1989: 59).

As the myth just cited illustrates, power comes from the possession of knowledge of the inner secrets of religion. Despite male chicanery, the main depositories of knowledge about Candomble have been and for the most part continue to be women. During slavery, while their menfolk were scattered throughout the sugar plantations, it was the women who, for the most part (as already noted) kept the knowledge of the myths alive, arranged and presided over the ceremonies, cured the sick and passed on the traditions to the next generation. Even today an enquirer is directed to the older women members for 'important information' about Candomble and especially for knowledge about its remedies. Landes wrote that although many of the intellectuals knew a great deal about Candomble, they acknowledged that the above-mentioned mae-de-santo, Mae Menininha, was 'superior to them all in medicine' (1947:85). According to Landes, Menininha was:

> the guardian of a religious philosophy ... and had the authority over hundreds of souls by reason of her knowledge (sabedoria) and priestly talent (ibid).

She also, as is the case generally with women leaders, inspired trust and confidence.

Moral factors

Some mention has already been made of male and female attributes, and here we can refer briefly to two other qualities – self-control and probity – which are mostly associated with women. Self-control in the sense of the ability to remain calm under all circumstances is perhaps the most prized of all the qualities deemed necessary in a Candomble leader. It does not prohibit firmness, decisiveness and even the punishment of wrong-doers. But it does rule out displays of anger and, even more, petulance, in public.

As to probity and moral integrity, it was pointed out above that it is through a rite of initiation that one becomes a full member of Candomble, and it was in relation to this rite in particular that informants spoke of women leaders being more honest and reliable than men. This is regarded as extremely important, for the leader alone has the right to visit and oversee the novice in her/his cell, and it was in the discussion of this part of the rite that respondents would single out women priests as being 'safer' than men. They also appear to combine great self-confidence and a 'monstrous' need to succeed with an abundance of charisma.

'Monsters'

Perhaps just as important in the creation of the priestess as the moral and other factors mentioned above is the crucial element of charisma grounded in an unshakeable belief found among many maes-de-santo in their own right and ability to perform this role better than others. Verger speaks of the need to be a 'monster to be a mae-de-santo'. (Verger Interviews: 1986-91). By the term 'monster' he means someone who is possessed of an extra-ordinary degree of self-reliance and a deeply felt need to succeed.

Considering the disadvantaged position from which the early founders and leaders of Candomble in Bahia had started and the heights to which they rose – not only religiously but also socially and politically – they clearly required an enormous amount of determination and self-assurance, which in a patriarchal society accepted as the norm by almost everyone including women, must have appeared highly unusual and even somewhat unnatural.

Two of Bahia's most famous priestesses were Mae Senhora of the terreiro Ile Ase Opo Afonja, (the powerful stronghold of Xango), situated in Sao Ganzalo de Retiro, a suburb of Salvador, the capital of Bahia, and Mae Menininha of the terreiro of Gantois, in the district of Federacao, which lies closer to the centre of the same city. Comment here will be confined for the most part to Mae Senhora.

Prior to becoming the Iyalorisha or chief priest of Ile Ase Opo Afonja, Mae Senhora made a living from selling fruit in the market. Verger, who was later to be initiated by her into Candomble, recalls that even then Mae Senhora's intentions were clear. Among other things she named her stall 'A Vencedora' (the Victor) and drank only one brand of liquor, 'O Vencor' (Verger interviews: 1986-91) For Mae Senhora no position, title or tribute was too grand or undeserved. This makes sense in one who believed that slavery was not only a negation of her self as a person but also the destruction of a once proud and honourable people with a long and glorious history and civilization of their own. Whether consciously or unconsciously, Mae Senhora strove to reverse the degrading consequences of slavery which deprived people of their colour of dignity, opportunity and power by rising high in Candomble, the only avenue of advance open to someone like herself who was a descendant of a slave.

Female priests, it is worth mentioning, are not necessarily feminists, or socially and politically radical, even when it is a question of black and white issues. While they support equality for all, they do not always accept the means advocated for achieving it and can even display what could be considered conservative political attitudes. Likewise, in the exercise of their power and authority within Candomble, they can be highly authoritarian in their dealings with their devotees. Possession by an African god enabled Mae Senhora to 'return' to the pre-slavery era, to ground herself, as it were, in the culture to which she felt she belonged and which later honoured her by conferring on her the title *Iyanaso* (see definition above). Verger's recollection is that Mae Senhora, on hearing that the King of Oyo in south-western Nigeria had awarded her this title, exclaimed 'Now I am my ancestor', a response that lends support to the interpretation of the purpose of possession outlined above (Verger interviews: 1986-91).

Although this self-assurance and self-confidence is not uncommon in female priests in present-day Bahia, charisma of the kind exerted by Mae Senhora, Mae Menininha and other well known priestesses generates its own momentum and survives long after their departure. The relationship between charisma and physical appearance is a complex one. On first impressions Mae Menininha appears to have been anything but charismatic. Although she possessed some very expensive clothes, Landes noted that she dressed badly. She wore a black shawl over her head and shoulders and the rest of her clothes were not particularly tidy nor even clean. She was also very overweight, had one tooth missing in the centre of her mouth, and the lenses of her spectacles were unusually thick. However, despite her weight, she was an outstanding dancer, possessed 'a strong, sweet contralto's voice', and 'spoke calmly and peacefully'. Menininha struck Landes as:

> a priestly figure dancing and reciting with soul the old and refined lessons of her traditions (1947:93).

Today, leading Candomble priests in Bahia, male as well as female, make it a point to rule in the style of such famous maes-de-santo and to adopt inside and outside the ceremonials, the same air and the same tone of voice and gestures as these once very powerful and much sought after priestesses.

Women as ideal devotees

It is clear that for historical reasons and on account of their own initiative rather than their gender women priests are in the majority in Bahian Candomble. However, women priests can also symbolically reinforce received notions of male power and domination, including a wife's traditional role as servant of her husband. From the perspective of both the symbolism of Candomble and the socio-cultural background from which it derives, a woman is clearly a more appropriate vehicle for the sacred, a more fitting vessel for the gods to incorporate in than a man for, as previously noted with reference to Verger, all those dedicated by initiation to the gods become their wives. Thus, the relationship between husband and wife in which the latter is subordinate to the former provides the model for the relationship between a god and his devotees.

Looked at from this perspective, Candomble is about submission to the will of the gods, about serving the gods by catering for their needs, especially by preparing their special dishes. Such service is widely regarded both in Yoruba society and in Bahia as the task of women. Symbolically the more feminine the devotional ritual is the better. This is similar to bhakti, where as O'Flaherty explains:

> The devotee visualises himself as a woman not merely because god is male but because in the Hindu view the stance of the ideal devotee is identical with the stance of the ideal woman (1980:88).

As already noted, men have the duty of sacrificing animals, particularly large animals such as goats, dogs and oxen for divine consumption, a task which, it is believed, requires the male attributes of strength, firmness and precision. There is also a widely held belief that menstrual blood is impure and can defile a sacrifice. Therefore, from the perspective of the liturgy of Candomble it could be argued that women are the priests not because they have some innate, natural capacity to communicate with the divine which men do not possess, but rather because they provide more potent symbols of the basic elements – obedience and submission – of the relationship that ought to exist between devotees and their gods. There is also an aesthetic element in this relationship, which in the context of local culture makes it more appropriate for women rather than men to be the priests. Candomble is theatre; it is the re-enactment of the adventures and exploits of the gods who are believed to be full to overflowing with desire and passion and who are attracted by the sensuous, the elegant, the graceful, the beautiful and related qualities, which are more often associated with women than with men.

Sexual orientation and participation in Candomble

Although the ideal devotee is a woman and although aesthetic considerations are of symbolic importance, it is misleading to suggest, as Landes does, that the only males who can meaningfully participate in the ritual dance at the centre of Candomble are passive homosexuals. This is not to suggest that she was entirely wrong about the sexual orientation of the male members; on this there are no reliable statistics. However, it is well known that heterosexual males actively participate in the ceremonies, though by no means all of them are priests. Many of the male members have the title of *Oga* (protector). Some play the drums, others perform the sacrifices, and others take responsibility for maintaining order and decorum during the services.

Furthermore, sexual orientation is of little relevance in principle to membership in Candomble. Leaders and participants in general may or may not look favourably upon homosexuality, but that is unimportant for several reasons. First of all, it is accepted that all devotees are what they are by virtue of their destiny, which is decided before birth. Moreover, it is the principal duty of their god to help individuals to fulfil that destiny in return for propitiatory sacrifices. Consequently, it would be a serious mistake for one devotee to arbitrarily interfere in such an important matter as another devotee's sexual orientation for that would be to interfere in the affairs of that person's god, who by way of revenge could inflict serious punishment in the form of an illness or unemployment on the wrongdoer. Moreover, devotees often model their behaviour on their god and, thus, criticism of an individual's sexual orientation could be construed as criticism of the comportment of their god. The sexual orientation of members is not in theory any more of an issue than anything else, for it is believed that the purification ritual performed prior to a ceremony by all those about to participate in it directly cleanses them of all fault. If, therefore, homosexuality be a fault, it is one that can be ritually removed for the duration of the ceremony.

In Landes' time it was probably the case that many homosexuals, and in particular her category of passive homosexual, found in Candomble a haven from the intolerance and exploitation of the wider society. Today the opposition to homosexuality is likely to come from the family and can lead people to enter what they perceive to be the more tolerant atmosphere of Candomble. Four informants between the ages of sixteen and eighteen, all of them practising homosexuals from between the ages of twelve and fourteen, explained that their homosexuality was unacceptable to their parents and that Candomble was a good forum for meeting others like themselves. Just as important to them was the fact that through its dance and music Candomble enabled them 'to feel the real rhythm' of their bodies, which was otherwise for the most part suppressed (Interviews: Recife: 1986).

In general, the majority of the male members of Candomble do not become involved in the dance ritual of Candomble, and the reason is partly that such dancing in public is traditionally more a feminine than a masculine activity. This should not be allowed to obscure the fact that dance also binds together all participants in Candomble whatever their sex, and in particular the drummer and the dancer. While allowing for a totally inner experience, dance is above all a communal and public event transcending natural and artificial divisions.

Conclusions

Any explanation of the high incidence of women priests in Bahian Candomble must, it would seem, pay greater attention to historical, economic, social, moral, aesthetic and liturgical considerations than to gender. This is not to suggest that certain qualities and attributes are not seen in terms of gender. As we have already shown, precision, firmness and physical strength tend to be regarded as male while submission, obedience, inner spiritual depth, elegance and gracefulness are mostly associated with women, and are certainly important assets in any Candomble priest.

Other requirements considered even more essential, while often associated with men, are in Candomble milieu said to be more readily found in women. The most important of these are: wisdom, knowledge born of experience, integrity, self-control and tact or diplomacy. Historical and economic developments underpinned by reworked traditions account for this association more than considerations of gender.

References

Note: This paper is based on fieldwork in Bahia and to a lesser extent Recife and Sao Paulo from 1986-91. I have referred to my interviews – ten in all – with Pierre Verger during this period as Verger Interviews (1986-91). There is also a reference in the text to an interview I had with four Candomble members in Recife in September 1986.

R Bastide (1960), *Les Religions Africaines au Brésil*, Paris
J Braga (1989), *Contos Afro-Brasileiros*, Salvador, Bahia: EGBA
V de Costa Lima (1984), Nações de Candomblé, in *Encontro de Nações-de Candomblé*, Salvador, Bahia: Ianama, pp.11-27
M J Herskovits (1943), The Southernmost outpost of New World Africanisms, in *American Anthropologist*, 45, pp. 495-510

D J Hess (1991), *Spirits and Scientists,* Pennsylvania: Pennsylvania State University Press

R Horton (1983), Social Psychologies: African and Western, in M. Fortes, *Oedipus and Job in west African religion* (with an introductory essay by R. Horton), Cambridge: Cambridge University Press, pp.41-87

R Landes (1947), *The City of Women,* New York: Macmillan also published as *A Cidade das Mulheres,* trans. M.L. do Eirada Silva, Civilização Brasileira, 1967

W O'Flaherty (1980), *Women, Androgynes and Other Mythical Beasts,* Chicago: Chicago University Press

Olga Francisca Regis (1984), Nação-Queto, in *V. de Costa Lima,* pp.27-35

R Farris Thompson (1984), *Flash of the Spirit,* New York: Vintage Books

W Valente (1977), *Syncretismo Religioso Afro-Brasileiro,* S.Paulo:Companhia Editora Nacional

P Verger (1985), The Special Contribution of Women to Candomble in Brazil, paper presented at the Sao Luiz de Maranhao symposium on 'Survivals of African religious traditions in the Caribbean and Latin America'

9

Charismatic feminist leaders in magic-esoteric groups in Italy

CECILIA GATTO TROCCHI

Among the more bewildering aspects of the kaleidoscopic cultural scene of Italy in recent years is a complex of phenomena which, for lack of a more precise label, has generally come to be designated as the 'occult revival'. These phenomena are also characteristic of other Western societies in Europe and in the USA.

There are also a variety of forms of popular entertainment dealing with the occult: American films such as *Ghostbusters* and *Ghost*, the Italian film *The Sect of Dario Argento*, and television series such as *Twin Peaks*. The second Italian network broadcasts a daily horoscope viewed by 12 million people. Lectures, courses and classes offer a full range of esoteric and mystical studies, from alchemy to Zen Buddhism. In Italy there are over 200 esoteric groups, with 30 to 2000 followers.

Occultism has been successful in creating a milieu, even if it is not very successful in organizing it. While Rosicrucian and other ancient wisdom movements do not have a very large membership, lectures entering the circuit of esoteric-occult clubs and meetings may easily attract an audience of a thousand or more in the larger cities.

Among the ancient wisdom movements new esoteric groups have been born and are still growing. I followed many of these in a sort of 'full immersion', using the anthropological technique of participant-observation. One of the characteristics of these groups is the presence of a charismatic leader. I will discuss four cases in which the leader is a woman.

Barbara

This group can be defined as 'magical'. Its master is a 50-year-old woman named Barbara. She is half Russian and half Bulgarian, and she likes to be called a witch. Her group is named Isis: School of Light and Realization. Around her is a legend created by her disciples.

During a relatively short but highly successful career as an actress in Italy, Barbara found that the stage was lacking one necessary ingredient: magic. So she left her position to devote herself full-time to spiritual and magical teaching. Her disciples relate that over ten years Barbara received direct tutelage from two masters of ancient druidic and magical order. Revelations were imparted to her at this time indicating that she should establish a school where men and women could develop their true potential 'for the betterment of the human race'. She married a young devotee who acts as her manager.

Barbara's teaching consists basically of the esoteric significance of such topics as: colour and sound, electricity and magnetism, mind-power, astrology, symbology, the laws of polar union, and different kinds of divination from tarot cards to coffee powder. In the higher classes she teaches white and red magic.

Barbara has 50-80 disciples. When I studied the school I found among them a Roman Catholic priest, two secondary school teachers, three television journalists plus some ordinary folk. There were more women than men; the age was from 25 to 60.

Barbara has great charisma. She is well educated, speaks six languages, and her Italian is perfect. She can be considered a feminist. She hates the Christian Church for its persecution of witches. She believes witchcraft was the ancient women's religion focused on a Goddess with different names as Diana, Pertcha, Holda, the Lady of Plants and the Lady of Beasts. During the Christian era the image of the Goddess suffered a deep and largely debasing transformation. Life-creating power once belonged to the Goddess alone; the Life-Giver and the Death-Wielder were one deity. The black aspect of the One Goddess was turned into a witch of night and magic. During the period of the Great Inquisition the Goddess was considered to be a disciple of Satan.

The dethronement of this truly formidable Goddess, whose legacy was carried on by wise women, prophetesses and healers who were the best and the bravest minds of the time, is marked by blood. Barbara has many books on witchcraft, including the Malleus Maleficarum ('the Hammer of the Witches'). She often said that the witch-hunt was the most Satanic event in European history, the beginning of the dangerous convulsions of androcratic rule and power, which reached their peak under Stalin's government. According to Barbara, Stalin ('the phallocratic one') instigated the torture and murder of 50 million women, children and men.

Barbara's charisma is based in her culture and on her enchantments. She has mixed a potent cocktail of feminism plus theoretical and practical magic. She prepares talismans and seals, and teaches ancient rituals of sacred witchcraft to honour the Great Goddess.

Once I took part in a ritual performed by Barbara and three other women. The occasion was the celebration of the midsummer feast of August, the period in which the Roman Catholic Church celebrates the Virgin Mary. Barbara offered to the Goddess homemade bread and white wine. She prayed with these words: 'Lady of life, Holy Earth Mother, She of the Corn and She of the Field! Accept our ancient rite of Love!' The ritual took place in the open air, in the woods near Nemi, not far from Rome, where once stood the temple of Diana Nemorense (well known through George Fraser's *Golden Bough*). Two women dug a small furrow in the earth where bread was placed, while wine was poured over it. Barbara said the last prayer. 'Lady of life! Be thou always blessed! May thou always be honoured and respected by all who owe their life to thee! Blessed be and blessed be!'

Elvira Giro

Elvira Giro was the oldest charismatic leader I contacted. She is an old woman of 80 and defines herself as the priestess of the Great Cosmic Mother (who is also the Virgin Mary). Elvira received communications from the Great Cosmic Mother through a personal channel in which extraterrestrial entities also participate. Her group is named 'the Cross Army of the She Holy Ghost', because Elvira Giro revealed that the Holy Ghost is the Parusia (manifestation) of the great Cosmic Mother, the Virgin Mary.

In her teaching Elvira uses Roman Catholic symbols and the religious ideas of a dead prophet named David Lazzaretti, well known in Italy because he carried on a large religious movement involved with socialism and political struggle. Lazzaretti died in 1878, shot by the Italian Army during a short but bloody battle in Tuscany. Elvira is in personal contact with the prophet, but she has improved the religious ideas of Lazzaretti with many personal insights. She combines Christian doctrines with some heretical beliefs such as the feminine aspect of the Holy Ghost – a belief of some gnostic sects of the third century A.D.

Elvira also combines together different esoteric beliefs such as reincarnation and its correlative tripartite model of human beings as consisting of body, soul and spirit. Reincarnation, in Elvira's teachings, is the belief that the soul passes from one body to another in a series of incarnated existences. She sometimes suggests to her disciples that they are the reincarnation of the Queen of the Universe, the Cosmic Mother, whom Christians call the Virgin Mary. She frequently speaks about the prodigious power of her left hand. Her knowledge is mythical, magical and theosophical.

In 1984 Elvira spoke to a Roman Catholic Cardinal named Ugo Poletti, one of the most important Cardinals in the Vatican. Very surprised, he asked her, 'But are you, by any chance, the Virgin Mary?' Elvira answered: 'It was you who said it'.

Camilla: Muslim prophetess

Camilla is the Italian representative of an Islamic mystical sect, known as God's Fervent Ones. Her family is numbered among the Roman aristocracy, whose stately palazzo in the city contains frescoes by Raphael and Guido Reni. The spread of the sect in Italy owes much to her personal charisma. She is also haughty and strong-willed, with stern yet captivating good looks. She is liberated and anti-conformist.

Camilla is spokeswoman for an esoteric group that has sprung up within an Islam that traditionally sees woman as subordinate and submissive. All wrong, says Camilla, for the way to the true liberation of woman is to be found in the teachings of Nur Ali Elahi.

The founder of the sect is a teacher from Kurdish Irna, who has kept alive a spiritual path that incorporates all the elements of Islamic mysticism. It originated in the Shi'ite branch whose own beginnings go back to the time when, following the death of the Prophet, the disciples of the Muslim gnoses gathered around Ali, Mahomet's son-in-law and first companion, who was an *Imam*. According to Nur Ali Elahi, as we may read in his book *The Way of Perfection*, after Adam's fall – Adam being the first Prophet – mankind has benefited from guidance sent from God. In the Semitic tradition, the people sent by God were first the Old Testament prophets, then Jesus, then, last of all, Mahomet. In other traditions these 'prophets' bore other names, many of them now forgotten. Some, indeed, were never known to men but were nevertheless initiated. These were the holy people beloved of God and entrusted with a spiritual mission. Muslim mystics – the true *Sufis* – know that they are indispensable intermediaries between God and man, and custodians of esoteric truths. These Wali constitute a spiritual 'church'. an 'Order', that sometimes takes on a temporal dimension but is not confined by any historical, spiritual or confessional limitations.

From the first *Imam* to the twelfth and last (the Mahdi) – Absolute Perfection was made manifest in each. Down the centuries they taught, in secrecy, the essence of belief and knowledge, while it was the adepts of the official dogmas that publicly developed the Islamic civilization known to all of us.   Upon the death of the last *Imam*, Shi'ism became a popular movement and gradually came to be an established, orthodox, esoteric sect within Islam, which now accounts for 10 per cent of Muslim believers.

Among certain highly reserved orders, the Sufis carry on the esoteric traditions and hold certain masters in high esteem; these are the Wali mentioned above, who have risen up from time to time in history. One of these was Soltan Eshaq, who in the fourteenth century founded this sect of God's Fervent Ones. The sect spread out into many provinces of Kurdistan. As time went one, however, some of its doctrines were lost or misunderstood. Now, Nur Ali Elahi has purged the Way of the Fervent Ones of the various accretions, spurious rites and deviations that had accumulated among the adepts over the centuries.

This master was the last-but-one of the secret teachers. Today, his son Shan Bahran Elahi is the head of the sect. He was born at Jehanabad, a village in western Iran, on 24 August 1931. He studied medicine in France, and it was not till 1963 that he returned to his native country and became his father's disciple. He was formally professor in the faculty of Medicine at Tehran; now he is in Paris and devotes himself to guiding his own disciples. He has published a text bringing together the ideas of his father and the fundamentals of the Way of Perfection, among them several of high spiritual calibre. After about a year of technical and practical training, the adept is ready for *salsepurdam*, which is a ritual whereby he abjures his former religion and makes his obeisance to Islam, binding himself to the way of life prescribed by the Koran.

Camilla's lessons are highly evocative and full of mystical atmosphere. There are perfumes and incense to sweeten the air, exotic refreshing beverages, and oriental music to lead disciples on in prayer. Camilla conducts these lessons for men and for women separately but exerts a powerful magnetism and dominating effect over both.

Carolina

Another esoteric group takes the name of its female leader. Its main centre is in a villa outside Rome, called Evo Cris, which was purchased with the contributions of the members, who now number more than 3000. Carolina is an attractive Mexican woman in her early forties. She is a lively person and imparts her occult teaching through mental dynamics referred to as 'levels'.

At the lowest level (entry fee 50,000 lire), Carolina teaches a kind of mental relaxation whereby the students are to be raised to 'level Alpha'. This is where positive thoughts are created and where one is enabled unfailingly to translate into reality. The powers of the mind are limitless: all depends on our thoughts. If our thoughts are positive then our desires will come true, whether it be a question of finding a parking place in the rush hour, getting a good job, coming first in a competition, being cured of neurasthenia ... there is no limit.

Passage from the first to the second level requires one to undergo a 'fidelity test' (fidelity, that is, to Carolina). This second level is the 'astral level', where one learns techniques of 'astral cleaning' and establishes contact with the Universal Mind. Spiritual retreats are required, lasting two days (and costing 300,000 lire), which entails a diet exclusively of fruit juice. When this second level has been passed through a second time, the adept will be able to effect cures at a distance. What is important is to destructure one's personality entirely, to achieve a *tabula rasa* purged of everything we learned at school or university; to unmask false masters and Catholic priestcraft; to heed only what Carolina has to say – to the effect that the truth lies within oneself and not in libraries. Among her followers are teachers, plumbers, students, housewives, civil servants, labourers, artists with quite a dab hand at 'destructuring' – all meditating for all they're worth from morn to eve and holding Carolina in saint-like veneration.

To pass to the third level requires a secret initiation. Here everyone puts on a white garment and fasts for three days with no solid food, meditating in front of a mirror, holding a white candle. In this way one achieves a vision of the Invisible Master – who may be Moses, or Jesus of Nazareth, or even some unknown personage. The powers of the adept now know no limitations (or so he or she is led to believe).

At the fourth level Carolina's voice changes. The adepts – as they will tell you (I myself did not venture beyond the third 'level'!) – descend into hell, where they are vouchsafed intelligence of unnerving verities. Travel, now, is in the astral mode, where one establishes contact with extraterrestrial beings. Carolina, one is given to understand, is one of their number.

This Evo Cris group organizes highly expensive trips to Latin America. It holds the theory that the cosmos is an emanation of the Universal Mind, and that Jesus is someone who has captured the 'Christ Ray', which is a mysterious cosmic energy, but something that anyone can capture.

Carolina refuses any meeting or interview whatsoever, and will have nothing to do with the press. My comments here are the result of my own personal 'initiation'.

In an appendix I described the technique as set out for the second "level" so that you can have an idea of the supposed logic of Carolina's utterances. However, under the surface, under the apparent differences of form, there one finds that the esoteric element is indeed the same throughout.

Carolina possesses all the characteristics of the 'spiritual director'. Her teaching involves successive stages; progress demands a test of fidelity to Carolina herself and submission to her Word. Her way of doing things smacks of mind control.

Disciples who reach the third and fourth levels display a devotion approaching idolatry towards her. Songs and poems are dedicated to her. Platonic (and not only platonic) love overwhelms these adepts, with whom she shares a life in common. They kiss the hem of her garment and weep at a kind word from her.

Unlike Barbara, who refers to ancient texts, or Camilla, who speaks in the name of Shah Baran, Carolina never cites 'authorities'. Her every word is the fruit of the enlightenment of which she alone is the repository. Carolina encourages a personality cult – encourages her disciples to hold her in admiration so that she can say to them: 'Do you like me? Well, then, if you want to *be* like me, follow my teachings'.

Exercise for the Carolina esoteric group

Planning

Always begin by relaxing your body, and then go on to mental relaxation. Your body will have dissolved away: instead of body you will feel a subtle energy filling your being. The confines of your body will become imperceptible; you will be immersed in the sublime force of the atoms of which your body is made. You may feel heat, or you may have the impression of a lowering of your body temperature. These are

all normal sensations accompanying the relaxation process. Some people sweat profusely as if invaded by some health-giving energy. In any event, the effects of the relaxation are beneficial. As you go on with your mental relaxation you will feel yourself going down ever deeper into your innermost self, until eventually you have no further sensation. However, the going down sensation, especially if localized in the head, helps the brain rhythms to slow down. Once you have immersed yourself in Nature, banish that scene and behold in front of you the perfectly clear and lively mental picture of what you desire - a picture that must be perfect down to the minutest detail, as if in that moment you were living the scene, putting your entire emotions into it.

If material things are nothing but the effects of movements of the mind, clearly the most sensible thing is to get at the cause rather than struggle with effects. The order of things is that an effect corresponds to the nature of the cause, and not that a cause can be changed by the effect. If you understand this principle you must be certain of achieving your purpose. This is because in the moment of imaging and intensifying the image you are constructing the scene or the circumstances you will later be living out. Remember: you are a creator.

The image thus vitalized is to be wrapped up in a layer of energy, so that it can be safeguarded from other thoughts that might weaken it. Do this and pass on the image to the Universal Mind. Your attitude must be one of love and genuine communication with this energy. Repeat mentally that you know that infinite mind is able to bring into being whatever is proposed to it. Now you must go over again the stages you have progressed through so far. Say to yourself: I am now properly relaxed; my mind is in harmony and that means I am in true communication. As I create the image I desire, I look into the fact and have the certainty that I am not violating any law of unity - what I am asking for does not violate anything and is not divisive in any way. I am violating no law of constructivity - meaning that I am not destroying myself or anyone else or any circumstance or thing. I am not flying in the face of the law of love - meaning that I am not asking for anything that causes damage or is lacking in respect either for myself or for my neighbour or for life, even. Being in harmony with the universal principles, let me pray that this idea of mine may come true. I am sure that I shall be living out the idea very soon, because I know it is necessary and beneficial for humanity, that it is constructive, that it is unifying and that it promotes the evolution of mankind.

You see, you have to be aware, when you are planning, that you are not controlling the universal forces but rather that you are guiding those forces with their own principles.

Once you are certain that you have placed deep inside the Universal Mind the image you desire, put your trust in the Mind and be sure that you will succeed. And since you are working in the present, at the mental level you are at, you must be receptive in the present, and be thankful. Thankfulness is a state of joy brought about by the realization that you have received something over and above what you had before.

It is interesting to see how anyone who doesn't thank doesn't receive - he may have possession of the thing granted but does not live the experience of the act of receiving, because he never realizes what cosmic goodness is. Thanking determines the degree of joy that you manifest in your life, because it indicates the amount of attention you give to things received. Realize that in this way you are loved and accepted by Universal *life* . The act of thanking gives you, among other things, even greater certainty of having received what you asked for. Once you have done all these things, you may slowly and in all tranquillity return to your state of consciousness and open your eyes.

The attitude that you must adopt once you have done this planning will be the same as the attitude of a farmer sowing his seed. The farmer examines the condition that the ground is in, removes any weeds, ploughs and puts any needed fertilizer on the land - and all proved he has the correct amount of water. Only when he has done all this does he sow the seed; he places all his trust in the sun, the air and water; and he knows these will bring his work to fruition. He has an absolute certainty in the laws of nature, and he is certain that he has not transgressed any of them, so he entrusts to them the carrying through of his work. In this way you will forget your planning, because once you have done it, it will represent for you something accomplished, and you will place your trust simply in the Universal Mind.

Do this exercise at least once a day, and in these same conditions.

This is all I am telling for now; but this is nothing when compared with what you have to learn. Put into practice these elementary counsels and you will discover that negative conditions, whether internal or external, are walls that must be pulled down, so that you can arrive at the threshold, at the starting point, of an eternal path that is within you, that unites you with the infinite Cosmos, and in so doing make you an *infinite being*.

10

Women and power in modern paganism

VIVIANNE CROWLEY

Undoubtedly

One of the most dynamic paths in women's spirituality today is that of Paganism.
Paganism takes many forms, but Pagans have in common a reverence for the pre-
Christian Gods of their own cultures and, in particular, that part of the divine which
has been long suppressed in Western society – the Goddess. In this chapter I will
explore the role of women in Western Pagan groups, drawing the conclusion that
Paganism, with its emphasis on the feminine part of the divine – the Goddess – has
much to offer women today.

Women's role in Western religion

Women's role in Western religion has been for many centuries that of follower and
subordinate to the male priest. In Christianity, women have been permitted to serve
God as nuns, but only recently has women's entry to the priesthood been even
contemplated. As people have become more aware of the importance of the feminine
in other aspects of society, they have also become aware of the lack of feminine input
in major Western religions. A character in Robertson Davies's novel *The Rebel
Angels* comments:-

> I like women, and the lack of a feminine presence in Christianity has long
> troubled me. Oh, I am familiar with all the apologies that are offered on that
> point: I know that Christ had women among his followers, that he liked to

talk to women, and that the faithful who remained with him at the foot of his cross were chiefly women. But whatever Christ may have thought, the elaborate edifice of doctrine we call his church offers no woman in authority – only a Trinity made up, to put it profanely, of two men and a bird – and even the belated amends offered to Mary by the Church of Rome does not undo the mischief (1981, 241).

Christianity has offered no truly positive and adult image of womanhood. The image offered by the 'Blessed Virgin Mary' is that of a non-sexual women who does not offer the threat that the sexual woman can pose for the insecure or celibate man. Mary is virgin; she conceives through a dove and, in order to serve her son, she lives in celibacy with her earthly husband, who is old enough to be her father. She has no will or purpose of her own. It is an ideal of womanhood that is safe and contained within the home by the son/husband/father.

The fact that in Christianity the acceptance of women priests is now being contemplated is, however, a major breakthrough and can be seen as part of a reclaiming by women of their religious rights to worship their Gods and to act as their mediators on an equal basis to men. This revival of women's religious role can be seen as part of a wider movement towards the active participation by women in all sectors of society – social, political, economic and religious. One manifestation of the change in women's religious status has been the thrust towards women becoming priests in the Christian churches. Another important strand is the development and emergence of Pagan Goddess-worshipping religions.

As yet, Paganism is a relatively new movement and few women are born into Pagan families. For most, the Pagan path is arrived at through a conscious decision by individual women, rather than through being raised by Pagan parents in their philosophy. Although it is of necessity a simplification, three major routes can be identified by which women come to the view that they are Pagans. These are feminism, ecological awareness and a desire for occult power or knowledge: the way of the witch.

Paganism and the Women's Movement

In worshipping the Goddess, men and women are reviving the religious traditions of the pre-Christian Pagan world. The return to Goddess worship is inspired by a number of forces. One is the Women's Movement, particularly in the United States. Since the feminist movement of the nineteenth century onwards, many women have been spurred to question the religious forms that have been familiar since childhood. They are turning to new spiritual pathways that lead not to the image of a patriarchal God, but to what is perceived as an older and deeper depiction of the deity: that of the Great Goddess.

For Christian women, this has often meant a questioning and rewording of their Christian liturgy. For other women, the search for the Goddess has led them to the distant past – to the Gods of their ancestors and to a return to Paganism. Most of the Pagan revivals in modern-day Western spirituality place a great emphasis on the Goddess, though some do not. The followers of the Norse Gods, for example, worship a strongly patriarchal group of deities. However, even in these groups the role of the seeress – the *volva* or *seidkona* (a priestess practitioner of magic and divination) – is of growing importance.

In its Information Pack the Pagan Federation (1992) describes women's spirituality as a very important part of the revival of Pagan religions in the Western world.

> Women's spirituality is one of the richest and most dynamic forces in modern Paganism. Women are respected in all Pagan traditions and have enriched Paganism with a powerful vision of the Goddess – the long-ignored feminine aspect of the Divine ... Drawing upon the inspiration of the image of the Goddess, women explore their own feminine mysteries. For some women, this involves a denial of all things seen as patriarchal; for others it is a spiritual calling to throw off the conditioning chains of society's stereotypes of women. These women see themselves as reclaiming or creating a new understanding of what it is to be female. They seek to bring their discoveries to life in their own lives, sharing this new found knowledge by way of myth, song, dance and, where needed, political action.

Some Goddess-worshipping groups inspired by the Women's Movement worship only the Goddess; often these are all-female groups. Many are groups of women meeting together on an informal basis and drawing inspiration for their rites from a variety of sources. Others would consider themselves part of specific Goddess-worshipping movements. One of the strongest of these, particularly in the United States, is the Dianic movement, named in honour of the Goddess Diana. These groups all have a matriarchal focus. Many Dianic groups exclude men and see their tradition as a sisterhood, as *wimmin's religion*. Others work with men, but see their role as less important than that of women. Many Dianic groups worship only the Goddess, and those that acknowledge the God see the male deity as a part of the mystery of the Goddess.

Ecological approaches to Paganism

Many men and women who have become deeply committed to 'green' issues have turned to Paganism and to the Goddess as an extension of their ecological philosophy. For these Goddess worshippers the Earth is Gaia, the Great Mother. A return to Goddess worship is seen as a necessary re-orientation of human beings' relationship to nature. It is a turning away from exploitation to a recognition of interdependence. This mutually dependent relationship is reflected in the songs and chants used by many Goddess-worshipping groups.

> The Earth is our Mother,
> We will take care of her.

> Mother Earth carry me,
> Thy child I will always be.

Nature is seen not as something wild and threatening that must be tamed, but as a nurturing and protective 'mother', who is herself defenceless and must in turn be protected. The relationship that is encouraged in Pagan philosophy between the Earth and her inhabitants is one of mutual protection and love.

Paganism and witchcraft

The third older influence that has led to a revival of Goddess worship originates in the occult revival of the eighteenth century, which inspired its followers to a return to Pagan religion. Initially these new Pagans turned to the Gods of Greece and Rome, familiar to them from their classical education and then to the Gods of Egypt, where archaeological discoveries had captured the contemporary imagination and uncovered a wealth of information about the Egyptian deities. More recently, the worship of other European Gods, such as the Celtic and Norse pantheons, has been revived.

In this movement *Wicca* – the name given by witches to the religion of witchcraft – has been the strongest influence. Wicca has in turn inspired much of the practice of later Goddess-worshipping groups, influencing both feminists and those turning to Goddess worship from an ecological standpoint. The rationale of Wicca is that witches are reviving an underground tradition of Pagan Goddess-worship suppressed by the Christian church. The witches persecuted during the sixteenth and seventeenth-century witch trials in Europe and the New World were not worshippers of the Christian devil nor solely victims of a witch-hunting paranoia, but followers of the indigenous, nature-based religions of Europe.

The divisions between those approaching Goddess worship from an ecological stance, a feminist stance, or through witchcraft, are, of necessity, artificial, in that many women who become committed to the Goddess through one route develop interests in other approaches to Paganism. This is evidenced by the approach of Starhawk, a witch and a leading figure in feminist-oriented Goddess spirituality in the US. Her book *The Spiral Dance: A Rebirth of the Ancient Religion of the Great Goddess* (1979) has drawn many women to take up witchcraft-based Goddess religion. Starhawk is also committed to radical action on ecological issues. Through her example, many Goddess-oriented women have been inspired to incorporate action on environmental issues into their concept of what it means to be a Goddess worshipper or a witch.

The weaving together of the three threads of ecology, feminism and witchcraft is apparent in a song that is often sung by Pagan groups: Charlie Murphy's *The Burning Times*, a modern folk song about the witchcraft persecutions of the sixteenth and seventeenth centuries.

> And the Pope declared the Inquisition,
> it was a war against the women whose power they feared.
> In this holocaust against the nature people,
> nine million European women died.
> And the tale is told of those, who by the hundred,
> holding together, chose their deaths in the sea,
> while chanting the praises of the Mother Goddess,
> a refusal of betrayal, women were dying to be free.
>
> Now the Earth is a witch and the men still burn her,
> stripping her down with mining and the poisons of their wars;
> yet to us the Earth is a healer, a teacher, a mother,
> she's the weaver of a web of life which keeps us all alive.

In taking radical political action in defence of ecological issues, many women have realized, perhaps for the first time, a sense of their own collective power: a power to stand against the male, patriarchal 'establishment'. Starhawk describes how she and

600 other women were imprisoned after blockading a weapons laboratory, and how they acted to prevent one of their number being taken away by the guards.

> The woman dives into our cluster, and we instinctively surround her, gripping her arms and legs and shielding her with our bodies. The guards grab her legs and pull, we resist, holding on. The guards and the women are shouting and in a moment, I know, the nightsticks will descend on kidneys and heads ... And then someone begins to chant.
>
> The chant is wordless, a low hum that swells and grows with open vowels as if we have become the collective voice of some ancient beast that growls and sings ...
>
> 'Sit down', a woman whispers. We become a tableau, sitting and clasping the woman as if we are healing her with our voices and our magic. The confrontation has become a laying on of hands.
>
> The guards stand, tall, isolated pillars. They look bewildered ... They do not know what to do.
>
> And so, after a moment, they withdraw. The chant dies away. It is over. For a moment, mystery has bested authority ... what has taken place is an act that could teach us something deep about power. In that moment in the jail, the power of domination and control met something outside its comprehension, a power rooted in another source. To know that power, to create the situations that bring it forth, is magic (1990, 4-5).

The collective power felt by women who act together is related to another aspect of power. Many women feel within them tides and flows of an intangible kind, which they define as 'power'. This power has been closely linked to women's menstrual cycle and hence to their sexuality; it has also been seen traditionally as the province of the witch. Even if they feel this inner power, women have little visible outlet for it. The exercise by women of 'magical powers' has been strongly suppressed and condemned by the male-dominated Church. However, the role model of the witch, closely aligned to that of the shaman, offers women the possibility of harnessing this power and of using it in positive ways to benefit humankind – to heal and to change that which should be changed. There is a chant devised by Lauren Liebling and Starhawk which is often used in Wiccan and other Goddess-oriented groups:

> She changes everything She touches, Everything She touches changes.

This is sung of the Goddess, but it strikes a deep chord for many women drawn to the Goddess and to the path of witchcraft.

The exercise of power is considered an important issue in Pagan groups. Many women and men who are attracted to Paganism are individualists who have reacted strongly against the usurpation by a priestly hierarchy of control of the religious function. Distinctions are often made by Pagans between 'power-over' and 'power-within':

> A coven is a group of peers, but it is not a 'leaderless group'. Authority and power, however, are based on a very different principle from that which holds sway in the world at large. Power, in a coven, is never power *over* another. It is power that comes from within.
>
> In Witchcraft, power is another word for energy, the subtle current of forces that shape reality. A powerful person is one who draws energy into the group. The ability to channel power depends on personal integrity, courage and wholeness. It cannot be assumed, inherited, appointed, or taken for granted, and it does not confer the right to control another. Power-from-within develops from the ability to control ourselves, to face our own fears and limitations, to keep commitments, and to be honest. The sources of power are unlimited. One person's power does not diminish another's; instead, as each covener comes into her own power, the power of the group grows stronger (Starhawk 1979, 37).

Power-over is seen as negative and destructive. Power-within, implying individuals developing a sense of their own inner strength, is encouraged. Although in Wicca-oriented groups the terms 'high' priest and 'high' priestess may be used, all group members are considered priests or priestesses. There is no gap between celebrant and worshipper; they are one and the same. In most Pagan groups all participants are involved in conducting the rites. Sometimes the extent of their role will vary accordingly to their experience, sometimes not.

Women's role in modern Paganism

Modern Paganism is different from most religions in that it accords very high status to women. Some feminist writers assume that Goddess-worshipping religions necessarily accord a high religious status to women, but this is not always the case. In many cults Goddesses have been worshipped by male priests, leaving no priestess role for women to perform. The high status of women in Paganism is derived from the theology of modern Pagans, who see the Goddess as *prima inter pares* of the Gods. It is She who creates the universe. Pagans worship both male and female deities, but it is the Goddess who receives the greater emphasis and who attracts many women and men to Paganism.

In all-female groups it is inevitably women themselves who act as celebrants of their rites. However, in mixed-sex Goddess-worshipping groups, women also normally play the major role. In Wicca it is the high priestess who is ultimately in charge of the rituals and the magic circle; this reflects the relationship of the Goddess and God to most Pagans. The Goddess is considered the origin, the creatrix; the God springs forth from her as her son, and in adulthood becomes her lover. This concept of the Goddess-God relationship is described by Bachofen in his study of *Mother Right* as meaning that it existed before human beings were aware of the role of the father in procreation (1967).

Some Pagan groups are formal and closed groups, and can only be joined through an initiation ceremony; others are more eclectic and spontaneous. Where initiation is practised, it is considered a rebirth into the world of the Goddess and the Goddess community. In all-female groups, these rites are performed by women for women.

Mixed-sex groups usually draw much of their inspiration from Wiccan ritual even if they do not consider themselves exclusively Wiccan. In these groups initiation is carried out woman-to-man and man-to-woman. A female initiate is initiated by the high priest, but the presence and participation of the high priestess is considered essential for the initiation to be valid. The importance of the Goddess is reflected in the limitations of the high priest's and high priestess's roles. The Goddess can create without the God, but the God cannot create without the Goddess.

The importance of the female role is also emphasized in the relationships between the various covens. Some covens spring up spontaneously, but most are set up by members of initiatory traditions who 'hive off' from the parent coven to form their own group. In these groups the concept of the religious community as family is very important. The coven is the immediate family. The coven members refer to one another as brothers and sisters, and the high priest and high priestess who conduct the initiation rites are often seen as 'spiritual parents'. *Lineage* is also important. In traditional covens inheritance is matrilinear. In many groups, even though women are initiated by the high priest, if he and the high priestess come from different parent covens the female initiates will trace their initiatory lineage back through the high priestess.

In most witchcraft rituals many aspects of the ritual serve to emphasize the importance of the feminine. Wiccan practice consists of worshipping the Gods at eight seasonal festivals, spread at six to seven-week intervals throughout the year and also at thirteen full moon celebrations, known as *esbats*. Rituals take place in a magic circle where the Goddess and the God are invoked and spells are cast. In all these activities the role of the woman is paramount. Traditionally the magic circle can be cast only by a woman. Since to cast a circle is to create, to make sacred space where none existed before, this is considered the prerogative of the priestess. In casting the circle the priestess is assisted by a priest, but he acts in a subordinate role. His task is to pass to the priestess the magical *tools*, the ritual knife and sword, which she uses to draw the circle and to call upon the presence of the Lords of the Elements who traditionally guard the cardinal points.

A woman is first presented with the *magical weapons* at the end of her initiation ceremony. These include the ritual knife and in some groups a sword, which are used to cast the magic circle. She is told that with the sword in her hand she is 'mistress of the circle'. To a woman, unaccustomed to the handling of weapons, their use gives her a strong sense of empowerment.

Pagan ritual often centres around *invocation*, a process by which the Goddess or God will temporarily incarnate in the body of a selected worshipper - a priestess if the deity is the Goddess, a priest if the deity is the God. Both Goddess and God may be invoked in the rites, but traditionally only the Goddess speaks what is known as a *charge*. A charge is a ritual utterance that conveys a message from the deity to the worshipper. Some charges are drawn from traditional sources; others are written by a group member or spoken spontaneously.

In the Wiccan initiation ceremony, the invocation of the Goddess is followed by the priestess who incarnates Her saying *The Great Mother Charge*. This conveys to the new initiate much about the Goddess and the importance of the feminine. She learns that the Goddess is 'Queen of all Witcheries', that from Her 'all things proceed' and to Her 'all things must return'. This emphasis on the feminine is in marked contrast to the religious liturgy that most Western women will have heard if they have been practitioners of Christianity, Judaism or Islam.

In the Catholic mass, the heart of the mystery is transubstantiation. The theological interpretations of the process vary according to the denomination involved, but in the interpretation of the Catholic Church, the priest becomes God and transfers his divine power into the bread and wine, which then itself become God. In this traditional interpretation women are excluded from performing the rite; they cannot become the male God. In Wicca the deity can incarnate in both priestess and priest, and it is the presence of the deity incarnate in the priestess – the Goddess – that is considered essential in most rites.

Women, men and power in witchcraft

All religions offer role models for human beings to follow, often in the lives of holy women and men. The role model for the new female initiate into Wicca is overtly that of the high priestess, but much of her understanding of the female role in Wicca will be derived more subtly from dramatized myths and legends of the Goddess and her relationship with humanity and with the God. Both the role of the priestess and of the Goddess in relation to the God are manifestly roles of power. It is the priestess who is in control of the ritual and is the ultimate arbiter of what magical spells shall be performed. The rite ends with a communion: Cakes and Wine. These are blessed by a priestess while a priest kneels before her to offer them to her.

Unlike outside society, Wiccan covens tend to see women as particularly suited to the exercise of authority in a group situation. The pre-eminence of the high priestess is considered essential to the success of the group. The witches Janet and Stewart Farrar give dire warnings of what is likely to occur if a coven is male-dominated:

> The High Priestess is the leader, with the High Priest as her partner; he acknowledges her primacy and supports and complements her leadership with the qualities of his own polarity. Leadership is required from him too in his own way ... The one thing he should not do is to assume the primacy himself ... We have known at least three covens ... which were dominated by the High Priest ... Two of them sank without trace, and in the other one the High Priestess picked up the pieces and began again successfully with a new High Priest. However much drive and enthusiasm a High Priest has, he *must* channel it through the leadership of his High Priestess (Farrar 1984: 181-2).

In Wiccan Law the initiate learns that:

> The High Priestess shall rule her Coven as the representative of the Goddess. And the High Priest shall support her as the representative of the God. And the High Priestess shall choose who she will, be he of sufficient rank, to be her High Priest. For, as the God himself kissed her feet in the five-fold salute, laying his power at the feet of the Goddess because of her youth and beauty, her sweetness and kindness, her wisdom and justice, her humility and generosity. So he resigned all his power to her (Johns 1969:135).

The rationale for the importance of the female role is derived from a ritual known as *The Legend of the Goddess*. This is a mystery play that is enacted when a woman undergoes the further initiation ceremony that makes her a high priestess and enables her to form her own coven. In *The Legend of the Goddess*, the new high priestess enacts the role of the Goddess and undertakes a 'heroic quest', whereby she descends into the Underworld and confronts the force of death (depicted as male) and overcomes it. She learns that when the Goddess descended into the Underworld:

> Such was her beauty, that Death himself laid down his sword and crown at her feet (Farrar 1984:29).

The sword and crown are seen as symbols of power and legitimate authority, and are given by the God to the Goddess. Power and legitimate authority therefore belong to her, not him. This symbolic gesture recognizes the underlying reality of male-female relations: the greater physical strength of the male. The woman can only rule because the man permits her to do so. In Wicca, he does.

When couples enter Pagan groups where women have powerful roles, some adjustments may be necessary in the relationship:

> If we enter Wicca as with our partners as many people do, there may be changes in our relationships with one another. Men who have been used to being the successful and dominant partner in a relationship may well find that their partner is much better at magic than they are and quickly gains an intuitive understanding of Wicca which they initially lack. In Wicca, women have a high status and for some women, it may be a new departure to be treated in this way and the dangers to the ego are obvious. Very masculine men may also find some difficulties at first in adjusting to not being treated as a superior sex. If a couple has been accustomed to playing stereotyped male/female sex roles, their relationship will have to adjust to the new status which Wicca accords women (Crowley 1989:80).

Some literature assumes that the Goddess is primarily a deity for women and that there are many all-female Goddess-worshipping groups. However, despite the prominence given to women in this religious framework, the religion was largely popularized by two men – Gerald Gardner and Alex Sanders – and, until recent years, men formed the largest group within it. This has changed a great deal now that witchcraft has become associated with the feminist revolution and the word *witch* has become a power word for women.

In recent years the Women's Movement has been counter-balanced by the growing Men's Movement, which has sought to redefine the male role in the light of changes in society and changing demands by women. Great interest has been shown in the publication of Robert Bly's book *Iron John* (1991). Central to Bly's argument is that initiation of men is something that must be carried out by men: 'Only a man can make a man'.

This belief is very different from that of most mixed-sex Goddess-worshipping groups. These groups, while not denying the importance of the male role model for men, convey the message that a woman initiates and that a man can only learn to take his full role in society by coming into right relationship with the female. It is not that woman is teaching man to become a 'New Man' and to learn feminine qualities, but to use the attributes of his maleness for the good of the community, to protect and to serve it. This harks back to the Celtic tradition of a young male warrior going to a female warrior for the final part of his training in weapons. In the Norse traditions women are also seen as essential instructors of men. Freya Aswynn, a leading volva in the Northern tradition, comments:

> It was the wise woman's function to teach magical practices to men, as well as to advise them in ethical matters. In this respect there is a similarity to the older continental tradition where women arbitrated in legal disputes and gave advice in councils of war (1988:194-5).

The message in modern Paganism is that it is the role of the priestess – and of woman – to guide society and to summon man to take up his male role.

The practice of the initiation of men by women is present in many Pagan rites, particularly those of Midsummer and Lammas, the time of the corn harvest. Ritual practices vary between groups, but Midsummer often celebrates the God taking on his role as King and protector of the people. Interestingly, the God may be seen as taking on this role with reluctance. He is persuaded to accept it by the Goddess who is pregnant with their child. She calls the God to:

> ... leave the greenwood of your youth and bear the burdens of a King and Man (Crowley 1989).

But the God fears to sacrifice his youthful freedom:

> I married thee, my Love, and not thy land.
> I roam the woodland wild,

the deer my companions and the birds my friends.
The greenwood is my home and not the seat of kings.
(Crowley 1989:178).

It is only through his love of the woman and their child that he is persuaded to sacrifice his youthful wildness for the confinement that accompanies the power inherent in the full male social role.

Women, power and Paganism

Worship of the Goddess in Pagan groups leads women to internalize those qualities associated with the Goddess. In the Pagan view the Goddess represents truths about their own essential natures for the women who follow Her. The psychological nature of religious experience is more overt in Pagan literature than in that of most Western religions and much of what the Pagan Goddess offers is explicitly psychological. Janet and Stewart Farrar explain:

> Now the purpose of Wicca, as a religion, is to integrate conflicting aspects
> of the human psyche with each other (Farrar 1984:146).

The Goddess in modern Paganism is visualized as Gaia, the Earth itself, and as immanent in creation. She is also conceived as the creatrix of the universe who pre-exists and transcends Her creation, the world of matter. The transcendent aspect of the Goddess provides women with a sense of an inner self as an unchanging core in the midst of the cyclical changes of life. By temporarily incarnating the deity in rites through the practice of invocation, a woman is not considered to be possessed (that is manifesting an external entity), but to be manifesting her own essential nature. Many Western religions accept the idea of an immortal spiritual component to the human self, but this is not necessarily believed to be of the same nature as the divinity. Modern Paganism takes the approach of the classical Pagan mystery religions:

> ... in the Pagan mystery cults, ... the neophyte, after initiation, is himself
> lifted up to divine status: at the conclusion of the consecration rites in the
> syncretistic Isis mysteries he was crowned with a crown of palm leaves, set
> up on a pedestal, and worshipped as Helios (Jung 1967:86-7).

Jung saw this as offering enormous psychological pay-offs to the devotee:

> To carry a god around in yourself means a great deal; it is a guarantee of

happiness, of power, and even of omnipotence, in so far as these are attributes of divinity (ibid).

Jung believed that by temporarily identifying with a particular God or Goddess archetype, the worshipper would be led to a true understanding of the nature of the Gods: that they are not external beings but powerful inner forces. This realization was a necessary step in the process of *individuation*, the term Jung used for what he saw as the primary goal of the healthy human psyche: the permanent healing of the division between ego and self (1968:113-15).

Coming into contact with a stable and enduring centre enables women to order their lives better and to come to terms with their emotions, conflicts and impulses. For a woman the Goddess is a symbol of the wholeness that lies beyond the confines of the ego. The Goddess is ultimately the Self: that to which a woman aspires and that which she essentially is. However, in order to find the Self, women must first have a strong ego. Demaris Wehr, Professor of Psychology of Religion at Boston University, argues that many women today have had their egos undermined by the low value that society places on the feminine, and that vesting divine power in a masculine 'God' reinforces women's internalization of this oppression (1988).

In Pagan groups, women learn to value the feminine and where necessary grow and nurture their undervalued egos. Through experiencing a sense of power and control they can learn to free themselves of the ego's grip. One of the most important things that Paganism teaches a woman is a sense of control over her own destiny, which she may not have learned in the outer world.

> Sexism consists of limited beliefs about the 'natures' of women and men ... it is particularly wounding to women because women are the ones who stand outside the definition of the fully human ... Because this is ... reinforced constantly ... in religion, in psychology, in popular culture – women find many difficulties in claiming adult status, responsibility, authority (Wehr 1988:15).

In the magic circle, a sacred space cast anew for each rite, it is woman who has ultimate power. In taking on the role of priestess, a woman demonstrates for herself her own inner power and provides other women with a much needed role model of strong womanhood to which they can aspire. When she has experienced this sense of power, a woman's ego can become strong and from this position of strength she can move forward. There is a song composed by Will Shepardson and the women of Greenham

Common Peace Camp in England, which is often sung at Pagan gatherings:

> We are old people,
> We are a new people,
> We are the same people,
> Stronger than before.
>
> I am a strong woman,
> I am a story woman,
> I am a healer,
> My soul will never die.

The image of women offered by Paganism is one of wholeness, strength, and other positive qualities that have traditionally been monopolized by men: Word, Power, Meaning and Deed (Jung 1957:20) By absorbing these qualities and by developing self-confidence and a sense of female identity, women are better able to become integrated into society. They are also better able to form relationships with men and to understand the role a woman can play in assisting a man to claim his manhood.

Myths often celebrate the hero's journey, the heroic quest. This quest is present in many of the myths and symbols of Paganism and it is undertaken by women as well as men. Demaris Wehr argues that:

> Symbols have both psychological and political effects, because they create the inner conditions ... that lead people to feel comfortable with or to accept social and political arrangements that correspond to the symbol system (1988:22).

By working with the symbolism of Goddess-oriented religion, women are led to reject social and political philosophies and systems that oppress them, and to seek social roles through which they can function as whole human beings.

Paganism offers many women a spiritual path through which they can honour the feminine aspect of the divine and play a full role as priestesses and celebrants of the mysteries of the Goddess. It is a role that offers power rather than discipleship and that helps women to internalize the qualities of the Goddess rather than demanding subordination to a male God. This power does not consist in power over others but in inner energy and strength: it is power-within.

Women's realization of inner strength benefits not only their spiritual lives but also their functioning in outer society. Paganism honours the Goddess as Mother, but also as Wise Woman and Woman of Power. Women are enjoined not to be passive vessels at the disposal of men, but in control of their own destiny:

> Priestesses in their own right, strong and proud, with their own vision.
> (Pagan Federation 1992).

References

Freya Aswynn (1988), *Leaves of Yggdrasil,* London

J J Bachofen (ed) (1967), *Myth, Religion and Mother Right,* Bollingen Series LXXXIV, Princeton: Princeton University Press

Robert Bly (1991), *Iron John: A Book about Men,* Shaftesbury: Element

Vivianne Crowley (1989), *Wicca: The Old Religion in the New Age,* Wellingborough: Aquarian

Robertson Davies (1981), *The Rebel Angels,* Harmondsworth:Penguin

Janet and Stewart Farrar (1984), *The Witch's Way,* London: Hale

June Johns (1969), *King of the Witches: The World of Alex Sanders,* London: Pan

Carl Jung (1967), *Symbols of Transformation,* London: RKP

Carl Jung (1968), *Archetypes of the Collective Unconscious,* London: RKP

Emma Jung (1957), *Animus and Anima: Two Essays,* Zurich: Spring Publications

Pagan Federation (1992), *The Pagan Federation Information Pack,* London: Pagan Federation

Starhawk (1979), *Spiral Dance: A Rebirth of the Ancient Religion of the Great Goddess,* San Francisco: Harper & Row

Starhawk (1990), *Truth or Dare: Encounters with Power, Authority and Mystery,* San Francisco: Harper & Row

Demaris Wehr (1988), *Jung and Feminism: Liberating Archetypes,* London: Routledge

Index

STUDIES IN WOMEN AND RELIGION